Classic Christian Realism
(CCR)

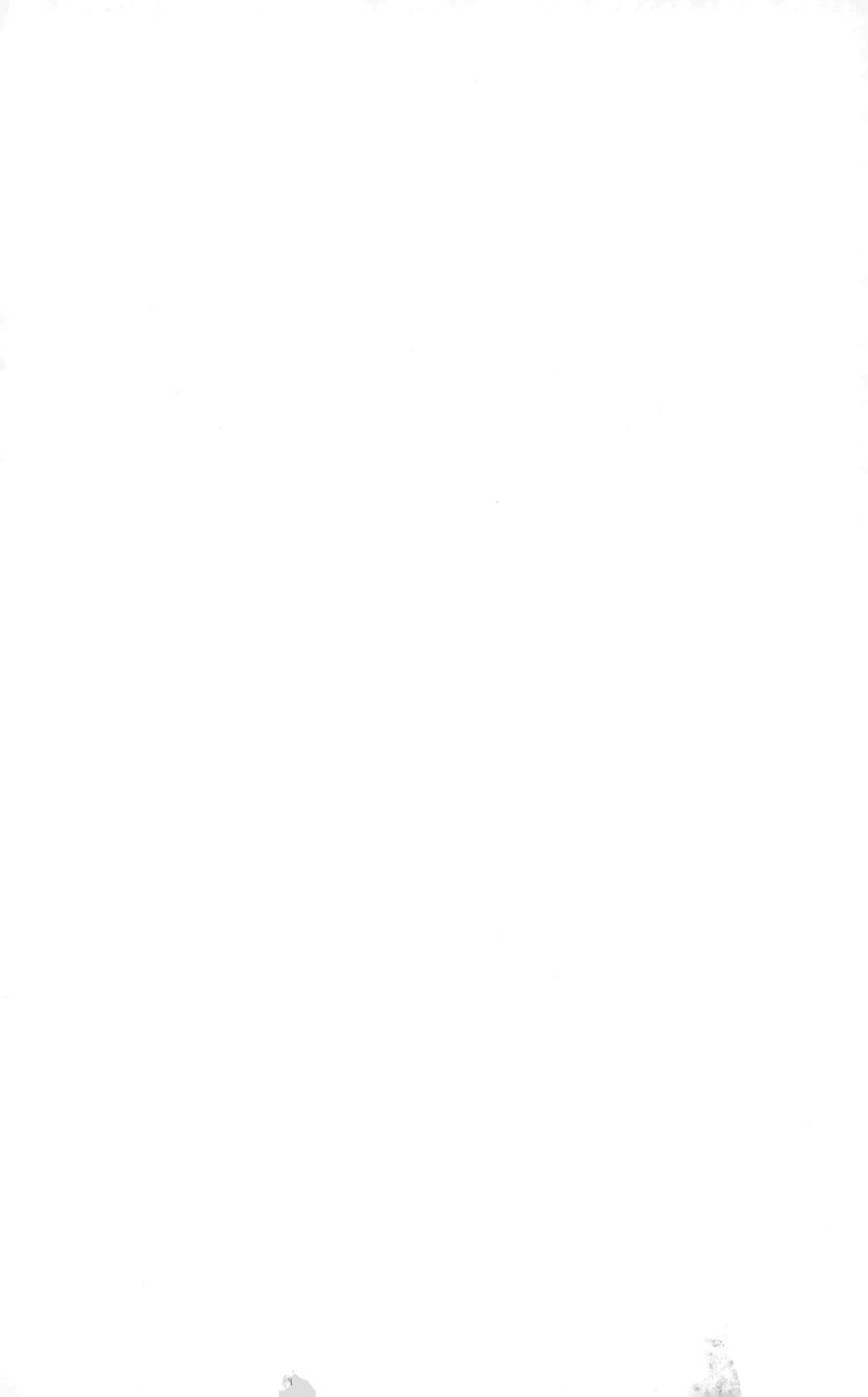

CLASSIC CHRISTIAN REALISM (CCR)

An Honest and Candid Perspective on Reality

DALE K. PACE

XULON PRESS

Xulon Press
2301 Lucien Way #415
Maitland, FL 32751
407.339.4217
www.xulonpress.com

Xulon
PRESS

Printed in the United States of America.

ISBN-13: 9781545624272

TABLE OF CONTENTS

ACKNOWLEDGEMENTS

I THANK GOD FOR the gracious salvation He provided by the death and resurrection of Jesus, and for the interest (and I hope insight) that He has given me in the topics addressed by this book. I am grateful for Andrea, my wife, who puts up with me and encourages me in things I undertake. A score of people have commented on material in the book or about preliminary things related to the book. Their comments and suggestions have been helpful in organizing the material and encouraged me to provide adequate explanation and support for ideas presented so the material can be understood more clearly. Reviewers were particularly helpful. They fact-checked historical statements and my scientific and technical comments; they also identified things not stated clearly and typos that needed to be corrected. I have not identified these people since there may be adverse reactions to things I say in the book. Those commenting or reviewing might be assumed to have similar views to mine whether or not they do. So I leave them unidentified but acknowledge that they helped significantly. I am the only one responsible for what the book says. Do not think anyone else shares an opinion expressed in the book unless that person has said so publicly elsewhere.

The three pictures on the cover of this book were photographed by Lynn Kochis of Camera Work Images (Woodstock, Maryland). The picture on the front cover was painted in 1962 by a man whose name I cannot remember. We were stationed at an Army base in Turkey. He hoped to become a professional artist after he left the military. While stationed at the base in Turkey, he spent his free time painting, developing his techniques; he used any surface he could get (this painting, 2 feet by 3 feet, is on plywood). I got the painting from him. Unfortunately he did not put his name on the painting and my faulty memory cannot recover his name after half-a-century; I had no communication with him after I left the army base in Turkey. Over the years, the painting has hung in my living room, in my office, and been stashed in the basement. It's perspective, that which one of the thieves being crucified with Jesus might have had, helps me to think more deeply about what Jesus did for me (and for all who accept Him as Savior). The picture on the back cover was painted by my mother decades ago. The picture normally hangs on the wall by my main desktop computer. It reminds me where to find reliable information about the spiritual aspects of reality. My mother, Elsie Pace, went to be with the Lord in 2014.

INTRODUCTION

D EVELOPMENT OF THIS book was driven by a con-
viction that Christians should be responsive to the prayer of Jesus
in John 17 for spiritual unity among His followers. I make no suggestions for how Christian groups (churches, denominations, organizations,
etc.) might overcome the organizational and theological differences that
divide them and limit their spiritual unity; instead I present a way that
Christians as individual followers of Jesus Christ can attain the kind of
spiritual unity demonstrated by the early church.

Hence this book is primarily for Christians who want to be responsive to
the prayer of Jesus in John 17. The book is also for all who think (or even
just suspect) that society dominated by materialism is missing something
important. Of course, others are also welcome to read the book.

Initially I planned to call the perspective presented in the book "Christian
Realism." Then I discovered that term had been applied to a philosophical perspective developed in mid-20th century by Reinhold Niebuhr.[1]
Consequently I added "Classic" to the name for the perspective presented
in this book so it would be clearly distinguished from Niebuhr's. "Classic"
is an appropriate addition to Christian Realism because the perspective
presented in this book is classic Christianity (similar to that of the early
church) and classic scientifically (similar to the ways that many great
scientists have approached reality).[2] No prior use of "Classic Christian
Realism" was found using the Google, Bing, and Yahoo search engines.
Thus I claim Classic Christian Realism is appropriate as the label for the
perspective presented in this book.

I thought I had completed the book. It had been fact-checked and reviewed.
I was ready to send it to the publisher. That version was about twice as
long as this book. It was much more informal. It was more like a discussion between two friends; at times it would meander off on extraneous

topics (such as unnecessary details and information about people mentioned which had no direct relationship to the topic of the book). Then I had second thoughts about the book's style. I wondered if presenting the material in a style more consistent with that of serious books would better help the book accomplish its purpose (that purpose being to encourage spiritual unity among the followers of Jesus and to suggest a more effective counter to secularism). After prayer and consultation with others, I decided that the more formal style and elimination of most of the extraneous material would be best; so that is what has been done. I hope that I have followed the Lord's will in doing this.

I share the above because of the book's emphasis on honesty and candor in dealing with reality. For that reason, I have included information about the author in the first chapter instead of placing such material at the end of the book. This will help readers to evaluate what I say in the book. In the same vein, the notes and sources cited in the Basic Works at the back of the book include materials (primarily websites) that are not considered suitable for citation in academic publications. I include them because I think they provide information that some readers may find interesting or helpful; but I do not vouch for their correctness (although I have not cited anything I considered unreliable or wrong). I trust the readers to use good judgement about what I say in the book and about what is said in citations. I am acutely aware of the fact that incorrect and misleading information may come from the most authoritative and best-informed sources as well as from the ill-informed or ill-intentioned. My years as an analyst in Defense matters made that very clear.

It is useful to note a fundamental aspect of reality that many ignore or deny, but which sets the context for this book. That fundamental aspect is that reality has a Creator Who has revealed how humans in His creation should relate to Him. Ignoring or denying hazards of reality is a common human trait. This is easily illustrated. Towns and villages are built at the foot of volcanoes and in flood zones. Cities exist in regions prone to violent storms. Similar denials of reality are common among those with addictions of various kinds.

Therefore it should not be surprising if significant numbers of people ignore or deny the Creator and His revelation of an appropriate relation with Him, even though doing such risks an undesirable situation for eternity. Such denial seems endemic to all kinds of people: intelligent and educated or otherwise; rich and poor; racially red, white, brown, black, and yellow; fat and thin; healthy and sick; etc.

In describing this denial of a fundamental aspect of reality, I avoided terms with positive and negative associations (such as "heaven" and "hell") so that the functionality of the issue would be presented without emotional baggage. However, it will be clear to the reader that this fundamental aspect of reality (the Creator and His revelation of the appropriate relationship to Him) provides context for everything in the book.

Finally, I thank all who read this book. I know that I am not a great wordsmith. I emphasis clarity about what I mean rather than clever expression of ideas, and that at times becomes boring. I appreciate the time and attention that people give to this book. I pray that God will bless them and hope that they will have the wisdom to believe in Jesus, accept His salvation, and live in ways that please Him.

Chapter 1.

REALITY

REALITY IS COMPLEX with infinite aspects. It consists of both material and spiritual aspects, and they can interact. Wise people accept reality as it is, neither treating only part of it as the whole of reality nor promoting an ideology at odds with proven facts of reality. Wise people accept observational and comprehension limitations of humans and contemporary technology. Wise people make a clear distinction between proven facts of reality and theory. This paragraph summarizes the perspective of Classic Christian Realism, which in this book will often be referenced by its acronym: CCR.

CCR approaches reality with honesty and candor. CCR approaches all aspects of reality that way. Approaching the spiritual aspects of reality with honest and candor enables CCR to facilitate spiritual unity among the followers of Jesus; that is a major emphasis of this book. Approaching all of reality honestly with candor enables CCR to challenge materialism for its failure to do the same, whether materialism is expressed in atheistic communism or in the secular humanism that has become so pervasive in Europe and America.

Complexity of reality is demonstrated by the fact that no single theory has been developed that can explain all observed physical phenomena. Instead different equations are used to explain observed physical phenomena at different scales, from the micro scale of particle physics to the macro scale of cosmology. Hence there are incompatibilities among contemporary explanations of the standard model used by particle physicists, the theory of relativity, quantum physics, and ideas about gravity. There are even differences in the number of dimensions assumed for reality by different contemporary explanations popular in scientific circles.

The complex nature of reality is greater than indicated by the above comment. Part of that complexity comes from the limited information about reality's spiritual aspects. Generally material characteristics of the spiritual aspects of reality are unknown. For example, it is not known whether atoms and subatomic particles have any part in heaven. There is similar ignorance about interactions between the spiritual aspects of reality and the material aspects. Generally a miracle by Jesus Christ, such as turning water into wine at Cana or giving sight to a man born blind, would be considered an interaction of the spiritual and material aspects of reality. Obviously atoms and subatomic particles are involved, but how such things happened is not understood. Atoms and subatomic particles are mentioned in the above discussion because later such will be mentioned in the definition of material aspects of reality.

Because this book is an initial exposure of CCR it does not present detailed examples from the material aspects of reality for such as noted in the above paragraph; nor does it point the reader to sources of readily available materials of general information. This book normally will only specify sources for quotation or specific points (and often do that just in the end notes).

That reality has infinite aspects can neither be proven or disproven. This is easily illustrated by a simple thought experiment. Think of how one might try to prove the number of stars is finite by counting them. Before invention of the telescope, that might have been a viable option. Only a few thousand stars are visible to the eye. If one counted every one of the stars visible to the eye, it would not prove that the number of stars was finite since one would have to assume there were no stars that were not visible to the eye. We now know that there are far more stars than the few thousand visible to the eye. Likewise any effort to prove reality is finite depends upon assumptions similar to the one that there were no stars other than those visible to the eye. The necessity of such an assumption demonstrates one cannot prove or disprove that reality is finite (or infinite). CCR assumes reality has infinite aspects. Such is an obvious assumption for anyone who believes God created all that is.

Infinite aspects of reality introduce conundrums, those difficult to explain things that do not make sense. In infinite mathematics, a line segment can both be thrown away and kept at the same time; that is totally impossible in finite math. Likewise there are such impossibilities that exist in reality because of its infinite aspects. Specific conundrums addressed

2

in this book mainly relate to spiritual aspects of reality and derive from God's infinite attributes.

CCR posits that reality has both material aspects and spiritual aspects, and that they can interact. This, like reality's infinite aspects, has to be assumed because it cannot be proven or disproven. Within the past century, modern science has realized that reality contains things which are not capable of observation by current technology. In fact, it is thought that the majority of the material aspects of our universe consists of such stuff. That unobservable stuff has been named Dark Matter and Dark Energy.

While Dark Matter and Dark Energy cannot be observed directly, its impact on what can be observed is evident. That impact is what led to contemporary postulation about Dark Matter and Dark Energy. CCR posits that reality not only has material aspects that cannot be observed directly by contemporary technology (such as Dark Matter and Dark Energy), but the spiritual aspects of reality also are beyond the capabilities of contemporary technology to observe directly.

CCR accepts observational and comprehension limitations of people and contemporary technology. Since human comprehension is limited by finite reasoning and expression, it cannot correctly explain or describe infinite aspects of reality fully; hence there will be conundrums beyond our comprehension. Only within the past century with development of the theory of relativity and quantum physics have the variability of things previously considered constants been appreciated (e.g., mass and time vary as velocity approaches the speed of light) and the potential impact of observation on reality begun to be understood. This leads CCR to limit proven fact (which CCR calls "certainty") to things established by direct observation with acceptably full explication of the method and act of observation; CCR considers everything else "uncertainties" (i.e., such uncertainties depend upon assumption).

This perspective is similar to that of Sir Karl Popper, one of the most noted philosophers of science in the 20th century. He distinguished between proven fact and "not-yet-falsified" theory.[3] Most of what is currently presented as scientific knowledge is in reality merely "not-yet-falsified" theory. Just because such knowledge is only "not-yet-falsified" theory does not mean such is not useful or generally reliable; the many advances in contemporary technology demonstrate that.

Modern science is based upon observational evidence and attempts to describe such mathematically. This uses mathematics to express theories about what reality is and how it behaves. Correspondence (or its lack) between predictions from the mathematics and observational evidence is used to determine the validity or lack of validity of a theory. Some seem to ignore observational and comprehension limitations by acting as if such theories can describe all that is. Others have a more realistic view.

Such a realistic view is illustrated by a comment from Richard Muller in his 2016 book *The Physics of Time*. "As for understanding reality, it is time to recognize that physics is incomplete. Physicalism has been a powerful religion, very effective in advancing civilization by the focus it has given to physics, but not something that should be used to exclude truths that can't be quantified. There is reality beyond physics, beyond math."[4] Dr. Muller is a well-known scientist, a professor of physics at the University of California at Berkeley. He received a MacArthur Prize "Genius" fellowship, as well as the National Science Foundation Alan T. Waterman Award "for highly original and innovative research which has led to important discoveries and inventions in diverse areas of physics, including astrophysics, radioisotope dating, and optics." In 2015, he shared in the Breakthough Prize in Fundamental Physics for the Supernova Cosmology Project.

The reader may ask, why this discussion of science in a book focused on the spiritual aspects of reality? The answer is simple. The above discussion sets the context for what will be said later about the material aspects of reality.

1.1 What is CCR?

Classic Christian Realism (CCR) is application of six basic principles to reality, applying the principles honestly with candor. The six principles are simply stated, and then each is discussed.

1) The first CCR principle: CCR addresses all of reality.

2) The second CCR principle: CCR applies the same honest and candid approach to all aspects of reality in its perspective.

3) The third CCR principle: CCR recognizes limitations of human perception.

4) The fourth CCR principle: Christian Scripture provides reliable information about spiritual aspects of reality and is the primary source of reliable spiritual information with general application to all people.

5) The fifth CCR principle: Key CCR tenets are based upon clear teaching from multiple passages of Scripture.

6) The sixth CCR principle: Christian responsiveness to the prayer of Jesus in John 17 is important.

1.1.1. First CCR Principle: CCR Addresses All of Reality

This is the most basic of CCR principles, and seems very simple (but that is deceptive; it is far from simple). This principle involves a specific concept of reality. That concept contends that reality is complex, contains both spiritual and material aspects which interact, and has infinite aspects. This book does not defend that perception of reality because CCR believes such attributes of reality are obvious. Certainly it seems to be the common conception of reality held by most people. Justification of this perception of reality is left to others.

The evidence that a material aspect of reality exists is clear to every sane person. That something beyond the material aspect of reality also exists is generally accepted by most people, although there are many different opinions about that something. However, there are a number of people that deny or ignore aspects of reality other than the material aspects of reality. Many labels have been applied to such people: atheists, materialists, physicalists, etc. Some claim that the perspective that nothing exists beyond material aspects of reality is a scientific perspective; but that claim is false because true science deals with what is, not what someone may think it is or wish it to be. An opinion about those who reject the Creator and spiritual aspects of reality has been around for a long time; it was stated in the Scripture by David about three thousand years ago: "The fool says in his heart, 'There is no God.'" (Psalm 14:1 ESV)

Hence the concept of reality upon which CCR is based has extensive general acceptance without detailed justification.

CCR addresses all of reality as it really is, which contrasts the CCR approach with perspectives which only deal with part of reality. Scientists and engineers know the folly of only addressing some of the parameters in dealing with a problem instead of considering all aspects of a problem if one wants a viable solution. That is why CCR addresses all of reality; a viable approach to life is best.

Many people innately sense that there is more to reality that its material aspects. This is illustrated by China. Since the communists came to power seventy years ago, the premise that the material aspects of reality are the total of reality has been promulgated. In spite of the forceful way the communists have promoted that idea, "hundreds of millions of Chinese are consumed with doubt about their society and turning to religion and faith for answers that they do not find in the radically secular world constructed around them. They wonder what more there is to life than materialism and what makes a good life."[5]

In addition, reality has many characteristics that bother thoughtful people. Those extensively involved in Christian apologetics have observed that many people have a sense that something is wrong with the world. That implies to them that God is either not powerful or not good, else He would have fixed things. This is a common obstacle that keeps many people from faith in Christ. Gregory Koukl makes this point in *The Story of Reality: How the World Began, How It Ends, and Everything Important that Happens in Between*. However, that is how things are. So that is what CCR addresses. Various Christian writers have wrestled with undesirable aspects of reality as they struggle with how a good and powerful God, such as described in Christian Scripture, could allow the abundant evil in the world. A classic example of such wrestling with that issue is *The Problem of Pain* by C. S. Lewis, first published in 1940.

CCR is candid in the way it addresses reality, acknowledging things that are uncertainties, even when they are extremely important. CCR does not claim something is a certainty just because it is critically important. History is full of wrong conceptions about reality, some of which have persisted for centuries after discovery that a conception was wrong. For example, geocentrism (the idea that the earth was the center of all things so that the sun revolved about the earth) is a prime example of such. Aristarchus of Samos, a Greek astronomer and mathematician who lived in the 3rd century B.C., wrote about the earth revolving around the sun and that the stars were like the sun but farther away. However, the misconception of geocentrism continued to dominate understanding of cosmology for most of humanity for about two millennia after Aristarchus. This was the situation until the ideas of Copernicus, Kepler, and Galileo began to take root in the late-16th and early-17th centuries; advances in optics that permitted development of the telescope helped their ideas to be accepted.

CCR does not claim insights about material aspects of reality beyond the generally known facts and not-yet-falsified theories of science and history. CCR's only distinctive trait relative to material aspects of reality is CCR's candor about the difference between what is really known for certain and what is only not-yet-falsified-theory (which CCR considers an uncertainty, i.e., based upon assumption or presupposition).

Misconceptions about the spiritual aspects of reality also existed for centuries; some of those ideas are no longer around (such as the Greek ideas of a human-like set of gods based on Mount Olympus), but there are foolish ideas about God that persist into modern times.

In addressing reality as it is, CCR recognizes reality's uncertainties as well as its certainties and is candid about such. This brief statement puts CCR at odds with many views of reality, especially in contemporary America and modern Europe where secular concepts have dominated public education in America for decades. CCR approaches reality as a whole, and does not present a mere part of reality as if it were the whole of reality. An approach that ignores part of reality is defective and deficient; but such is the approach characteristic of secular humanism and materialism.

Some falsely claim the assumption that God has no active role in reality, or even that God does not exist and never existed, is "scientific." The essence of science is insistence upon evidence for establishment of facts. Theories and assumptions are often useful, and may correlate with evidence yet still be theory. It is a great shame of modern education and of many in science and technology that they so carelessly suggest things are facts which are only "not yet falsified" theories. Their lack of candor in doing this reflects badly on their character or shows a careless use of terminology inappropriately.

1.1.2. Second CCR Principle: CCR Applies the same Honest and Candid Approach to All Aspects of Reality

CCR uses the same requirements for certainties with the spiritual aspects of reality as CCR uses with the material aspects of reality. Equal candor is presented about uncertainties and knowledge limitations in all aspects of reality. Therefore CCR makes a clear distinction between certainties and uncertainties in the spiritual aspects of reality as it does for the material aspects of reality.

CCR restricts certainties for material aspects of reality to facts demonstrated by measurements from direct observation with substantial information about the observation. Basically this restricts facts to measurements made within our solar system within typical levels of environmental factors experienced on earth, factors such as temperature, pressure, radiation, force fields, etc. Behavior descriptions summarized by various physical laws are accepted for ranges over which they have been measured directly; but CCR does not accept as certainties extrapolation of such laws to apply elsewhere. Such extrapolations are uncertainties.

Assumption that physical laws based upon measurements made by people and their technology in essentially a zero percent of space occupied by our solar system during essentially a zero percent of the time believed to have existed since the Big Bang apply throughout the universe at all times is indeed an astounding assumption. It is far more likely that those laws are modified at least in extreme temperatures, pressures, radiation levels, and other conditions postulated for parts of the universe (such as inside stars) as the laws of Newtonian physics were modified for mass and time by the Theory of Relativity when velocities approach the speed of light.

Because of limitations in human perception (as discussed in the next section), there are no certainties in the spiritual aspects of reality because measurements by direct observation with appropriate information about such measurements are impossible. Hence CCR treats everything of the spiritual aspects of reality as uncertainties because all is assumption based. To put that in religious terminology: it requires faith.

1.1.3. Third CCR Principle: CCR Recognizes Limitations in Human Perception

Human perception has two fundamental limitations. First, human perception generally cannot observe and perceive spiritual aspects of reality directly. There are also perception limitations in the material aspects of reality as well as the one just mentioned from spiritual aspects of reality. As previously noted, some material aspects of reality are not detectable by humans or current technology (i.e., Dark Matter and Dark Energy). Second, human perception is limited by finite reasoning and finite expressions (which prevent full and correct description of infinite aspects of reality).

CCR recognizes that it is difficult to observe spiritual aspects of reality, although impact of spiritual aspects of reality on the material aspects can be observed (such as the Apostle Paul notes in Romans 1 for creation); sometimes the impact of spiritual aspects of reality in the material realm is seen in the lives of people who are changed in some way spiritually and sometimes the impact is seen in what are usually called miracles (such as those reported in Christian Scripture: dividing the Red Sea so Jews of the exodus could cross, turning water into wine at the wedding in Cana, healing the sight of a man born blind, raising Lazarus from the grave after he had been dead for days, feeding a multitude from a boy's lunch, etc.).

The other limitation of human perception comes from the fact that finite reasoning and expression cannot fully and correctly address the infinite aspects of reality. CCR understands that reality has infinite aspects, which complicates efforts to describe and explain reality within the constraints of finite reasoning and language. Mathematics illustrates this conundrum: things that are impossible in finite mathematics are allowed in infinite mathematics.

Consequently characteristics of infinite reality may appear contradictory when addressed within the constraints of finite logic and language. Christian theology has wrestled with this conundrum for centuries. God has revealed Himself to be three Persons one Being. Somehow each Person of the Godhead is as much God as if the other two did not exist, and yet they are one God. This doctrine of the Triune Godhead, often called the Trinity, is never fully explicated by efforts to describe it. Similar conundrums present themselves with the dual divine-human nature of the Son of God, Second Person of the Trinity, and with the simultaneous truths of God's selection of those who would be saved before creation and individual free will in choosing to believe in Jesus for salvation.

Recognition of human comprehension limitations leads to the fourth CCR principle about where to find reliable guidance about the spiritual aspects of reality and to acceptance of conundrums in theology because the spiritual aspects of reality have infinite aspects.

1.1.4. Fourth CCR Principle: Christian Scripture Provides Reliable Information about Spiritual Aspects of Reality and Is the Primary Source of Reliable Spiritual Information with General Application to All People

Because people cannot directly observe spiritual aspects of reality generally, CCR assumes that the most reliable guide to spiritual aspects of reality is found in God's revelation contained in Christian Scripture. There are two major consequences of this perspective. First, this makes CCR beliefs about spiritual aspects of reality a matter of faith. This is consistent what the Scripture says about knowledge of spiritual things, such as found in Hebrews 11. Second, this restricts reliable information about spiritual aspects of reality to what is revealed in Christian Scripture.

This restriction of spiritual information to what Christian Scripture says is consistent with the perspective of a great twentieth century preacher, Dr. Martyn Lloyd-Jones. He accused the church of his time (mid-twentieth century) of superficiality, mainly for its failure to take Christian Scripture seriously. He said, "There is nothing more important in the Christian life than the way in which we approach the Bible, and the way in which we read it. It is our textbook, it is our only source, it is our authority. We know nothing about God and the Christian life in a true sense apart from the Bible."[6]

In CCR terminology, this perspective makes information about the spiritual aspects of reality an uncertainty since certainties are restricted to conclusive evidence based upon direct observation with substantial knowledge about the observation (things that Popper would call "proven"). CCR candidly acknowledges the uncertainty of information about spiritual aspects of reality. CCR not only assumes that Christian Scripture is a reliable source of information about spiritual aspects of reality; CCR also contends that Christian Scripture is the only reliable general revelation for all people that exists. Other revelation from God is more limited, and may apply only to specific people or specific situations.

This book does not present justification for accepting Christian Scripture as reliable spiritual information; there are numerous books available that address the reliability of Christian Scripture as a source of true information about God. A few of the more well-known works that address Christian Scripture as a source of reliable information about God are: William Whitaker, *Disputations on Holy Scripture*; John Owen, *The Divine Original: Authority, Self-Evidencing Light, and Power of the Scriptures*; B. B. Warfield, *The Inspiration and Authority of the Bible*, and E. J. Young, *Thy Word Is Truth*.

1.1.5. Fifth CCR Principle: Key CCR Tenets Are Clear Teaching from Multiple Passages of Scripture

As noted earlier, CCR considers information about spiritual aspects of reality an uncertainty because it is based upon the assumption that reliable information about spiritual aspects of reality is found in Christian Scripture. That assumption comes with uncertainties, as will be discussed in detail later in this book. Those uncertainties concern which books are Scripture, what is their text, and how should they be interpreted. Because of these uncertainties, CCR takes the following approach to provide a sense of certainty about spiritual truths. To prevent such uncertainties from corrupting perceptions of spiritual truth revealed in the Scripture, CCR restricts its key tenets (i.e., its primary beliefs) to things "clearly taught" in multiple passages from "undisputed Scripture."

The value of this approach is easily demonstrated. There are a number of small religious groups in the U.S. (more than a hundred congregations), mostly rural and associated with the "holiness movement," that practice snake handling in their religious services (this activity is thought to have begun early in the twentieth century). A primary portion of Scripture used as a basis for their behavior is Mark 16:17-18. Because it is the general conclusion of New Testament textual criticism that Mark 16:9-20 was not part of Mark's Gospel originally, that passage would not be used to support a tenet in CCR beliefs. CCR beliefs would not include such snake handling practices or beliefs about their role in Christendom. While this illustration comes from outside the mainstream of widely accepted belief and practice within Christendom, it shows clearly that the CCR approach of restricting key tenets to clear teachings from multiple passages of undisputed Scripture protects from beliefs based upon questionable passages of Scripture, interpretation of an obscure passage, or beliefs and practices that are grounded primarily in church tradition rather than in Scripture.

CCR focuses on clear teachings from multiple passages of undisputed Scripture. However, that is not an absolute limit on what one can properly believe. Some will establish beliefs and practices based upon things in disputed passages of Scripture or church tradition. Such may be appropriate if 1) such does not contradict a clear teaching from Scripture or interfere with compliance to clear teachings, and 2) such does not impede the spiritual unity Jesus prayed for. If any religious doctrine or practice not part of the clear teaching of Scripture contradicts any aspect of the clear teachings of Scripture or impedes the spiritual unity that Jesus prayed for, then such doctrine or practice is inappropriate and wrong.

1.1.6. Sixth CCR Principle: Responsiveness to Jesus' Prayer in John 17 for Spiritual Unity among His Followers Is Very Important

Instructions of the risen Christ to His followers were to make Him known to all people, and to make disciples of them. A few hours before Jesus was arrested and crucified, Jesus prayed for spiritual unity among His followers because that unity would convince the world that the Father had sent Him. In John 17:20-21, Jesus prayed "[20] I do not ask for these only [the men we call the Twelve Apostles minus Judas], but also for those who will believe in me through their word [which seems to refer to all who become followers of Jesus], [21] that they may all be one, just as you, Father, are in me, and I in you, that they also may be in us, so that the world may believe that you have sent me." (ESV) Their spiritual unity seems to lead to people believing in Jesus, which is an important part of what the risen Jesus told His followers to do.

This principle has significant implications. If one believes that being responsive to Jesus' prayer is important, that person will not allow other things to impede that responsiveness. This requires that a person keep his or her spiritual priorities in proper order. Secondary things, even when such are important, must not impede the primary things (worshipping the true God of Christian Scripture, accepting His salvation through Jesus, and being responsive to Jesus' prayer for spiritual unity among His followers).

CCR believes that the early church demonstrated such spiritual unity and that was a reason that God worked so powerfully through the early church. Contemporary Christianity is splintered into thousands of denominations, churches, organizations, and other religious groups, and some will not work with others in religious endeavors such as worship, evangelism, or spiritual training. CCR believes this splintered condition impedes spiritual unity among the followers of Jesus and may limit the way God works through His people.

CCR does not propose that a new religious organization be developed; nor does it suggest that Christians modify their beliefs if they are within the bounds of historic Christianity. Instead CCR encourages Christians as individual followers of Jesus to recognize the importance that spiritual unity has in God's perspective and take steps to facilitate spiritual unity with followers of Jesus. This requires that individual believers keep proper priorities in their beliefs and behaviors. Proper beliefs focus on God and His plan of salvation, and the importance that Jesus gives to spiritual unity. Those responsive to Jesus' prayer for unity among His followers determine not to let secondary things impede their promotion of truth about God and His plan of salvation, even when those secondary things involve important doctrines and important church traditions. This point is stated repeatedly because so many Christians, individually and in their functioning within churches and other groups, fail to be responsive to Jesus' prayer for spiritual unity.

If individual followers of Jesus will do what is suggested above, spiritual unity within contemporary Christianity will increase; this may cause God to work more powerfully through the church than He has done during the past century. The world desperately needs that.

1.2. This Book

This book is the initial exposure of Classic Christian Realism (CCR). It identifies CCR assumptions about reality and presents the six basic CCR principles. The book illustrates application of CCR principles to both the material aspects of reality and its spiritual aspects. The differences between certainties in CCR and uncertainties are explained and illustrated. Christian Scripture is discussed extensively since it is the source of reliable information about the spiritual aspects of reality. Key CCR tenets are presented.

Appendices address four topics with particular significance for CCR. Appendix A compares contemporary Christendom with the early church to show how powerfully God worked through the early church and to suggest why that may have been. Appendix B addresses spiritual unity to make very clear exactly what this book means by spiritual unity. Appendix C discusses *sensus plenior* and similar approaches to Biblical interpretation. Appendix D addresses impact on the church of social privilege and political acceptance.

The book has two primary objectives. First, to encourage more spiritual unity among the followers of Jesus because that is responsive to the prayer of Jesus in John 17 and because that may cause God to work more powerfully through His church. The world needs that desperately.

Second, to provide Christians with an approach that may cause some materialists to give more attention to God, or at least more attention to the possibility that there is more to reality than its material aspects.

Structure of this book is simple. This first chapter of the book discusses CCR's perception of reality and presents the six basic CCR principles. The chapter ends with information about the author and sections on perspective and terminology used in the book. The second chapter illustrates application of CCR principles to the material aspects of reality. The third chapter illustrates application of CCR principles to the spiritual aspects of reality and includes discussion the interactions between the spiritual and material aspects of reality. That chapter also addresses conundrums from reality's infinite aspects and discusses Scripture in detail since it is the source of information about the spiritual aspects of reality. The fourth chapter presents six key CCR tenets, and the fifth chapter is the book's conclusion. The appendices mentioned earlier, a limited index, and a listing of works cited or pertinent to topics in the book complete the book.

1.3. About the Author

Dale K. Pace is not a widely recognized leader in academia, theology, or philosophy; in fact, he's a college dropout with no undergraduate or technical degree. However he has a couple of graduate theological degrees (B.D. and Th.D.) and taught for a decade in a graduate program at the Johns Hopkins University Engineering School as well as taught an elective graduate course that he developed at the Naval War College. He worked at the Johns Hopkins University Applied Physics Laboratory for more than three decades, retiring from its Principal Professional Staff in 2005; he was a specialist in operations research. He has been involved in ministry to inmates for more than four decades, leading programs and ministering in jails, prisons, juvenile facilities, and halfway houses. He received the 2017 award from the Institute for Prison Ministries of the Billy Graham Evangelistic Center at Wheaton College. In comments on the dust jacket of a book Pace wrote long ago (*A Christian's Guide to Effective Jail & Prison Ministries*, Fleming H. Revell Company, 1976), Harold Lindsell (editor of *Christianity Today* at the time) said it was the "best book" he had seen on the topic and Myrl E. Alexander (former Director of the U.S. Bureau of Prisons) said it deserved "wide and full attention."

Perhaps this book on *Classic Christian Realism* also will be worth reading.

1.4. Perspective

CCR is the perspective of Classic Christian Realism. One of the definitions for "perspective" found in dictionaries is "evaluation of events according to a way of looking at them." This is the connotation for perspective in this book.

The CCR perspective is honest and candid, striving to view reality as it actually is. CCR contends that perspectives which assume only part of reality as the whole of reality are defective. This is the essence of CCR's complaint about materialism. CCR also contends that those who make exaggerated claims for a perspective are unethical. This applies to those who claim a perspective is scientifically proven fact when actually the perspective is only a not-yet-falsified theory. That allegation has been applied in this book to some exaggerating the perspectives of materialism and secular humanism. Such allegation also applies to some who make exaggerated proof claims for religious views.

The CCR perspective is based upon conviction that truth is important. The derisive question, "What is truth?" from a cynical Roman official, Pontus Pilate, is well-known. It is clear that truth was unimportant to Pilate since shortly after uttering that question he sentenced a man he knew was innocent to death as a criminal. Unfortunately many today seem as unconcerned about truth as Pilate was.

Is there an answer to Pilate's question?

The most substantial connotation for truth is correspondence with reality. That connotation transcends more limited definitions, such as agreement with a defined standard (such as logic and available evidence). Truth as correspondence with reality keeps truth from depending upon one's state of knowledge and from limiting truth to the constraints of finite reasoning.

It is obvious that sometimes truth can be hard to perceive. Conflicting evidence may exist. The situation may have aspects contrary to one's expectations. Aspects of the situation may not be known. The truth does not change, whether it is easy or difficult to perceive. Truth is what is.

The importance of truth is what makes CCR candid about uncertainties of its perspective. For example, CCR states explicitly that all statements about spiritual aspects of reality are uncertainties because they are assumption based. They all derive from the assumption that the Christian

Scripture provides reliable information about the spiritual aspects of reality. None of CCR statements about spiritual aspects of reality are proven fact based upon direct observation of things with full explication of the measurements involved.

Often the perspective one brings to things is a mixed bag of views that may not be consistent or coherent. These brief comments about perspective may help the reader to consider carefully and honestly the perspective that he or she brings to reality.

1.5. Terminology

Discussion of complex subjects requires attention to definitions and concepts used in the discussion; otherwise unnecessary confusion results. Reality is complex, and careful discussion of it and appropriate ways to approach reality require clear definitions and concepts if confusion is to be avoided. Below are this book's connotations for the terms shown for concepts which are critical to subjects addressed in the book, the discussion may be lengthy. Terms are listed in alphabetical order.

Autographs: the original manuscripts of Scripture, what the inspired writers actually wrote.

CCR: acronym for Classic Christian Realism.

Certainty: something established by direct observation and measurement with adequate identification of factors related to the observation and measurement conditions (full specification of relevant environment, by whom and how the measurement is done, etc.); everything else is an uncertainty. This severely limits what can be called a certainty. This perspective on certainty and uncertainty is similar to that of Karl Popper and empirical falsification.

Contemporary Christendom: Christendom since 1900 A.D.

Direct Observation: direct observation refers to measurement of something itself, not deducing things about that something from observations of other things based upon assumptions about consequences of interactions of the something with them.

Doctrine: a doctrine specifies belief in a particular area. For example, the set of beliefs about the nature of Scripture would be called a doctrine.

Usually a doctrine is related to a dogma (a belief about a particular point or topic), such as baptism. The total collection of doctrines for a particular group is usually called the "theology" of that group.

Early Church: the first two centuries of Christianity, from sometime in the 30s A.D. when the church began on the Day of Pentecost to about 240 A.D.

Infinite aspects of reality: reality includes God Who is infinite; there are no limits or bounds to His existence, presence, knowledge, or power. He is infinite in all of these ways. It is possible that there are infinite aspects of the material aspects of reality (such is implied by some of the multiverse concepts in cosmology), or the material aspects of reality may just be so large finitely that the universe appears infinite.

Material aspects of reality. Simple definitions say matter, the essence of the material aspects of reality, consists of mass and takes up space (some would add that it has inertia). Some say there are five phases or states of matter: solid, liquid, gaseous, plasma and Bose-Einstein condensate; others postulate additional phases or states (which may be called "exotic states"). Much of what some assume to be part of the material aspect of reality is not considered matter by modern science: these include energy phenomena and waves. Different parts of modern science may define matter differently. This book defines the material aspects of reality as anything consisting of atoms or subatomic particles (including point particles) — which the book will call matter including the corresponding antimatter and all forces related to them. The total combination of such comprises the material aspect of reality. This is as expansive as one can get in defining the material aspects of reality. It includes things like photons and light (which are outside the definitions of matter for some) as well as forces like gravity and electromagnetic waves. It also is compatible with contemporary ideas that are undecided about how many dimensions the universe (or multiverse) may have. However it does not include things (such as ideas) that some philosophers have speculated to possibly have an existence of their own apart from people. It is normally assumed erroneously that the spiritual aspects of reality is distinct from the material aspects of matter, although the two can interact; actually how the definition above (of atoms, etc.) for material aspects of reality relates to spiritual beings such as angels, the Devil, etc., places in spiritual aspects of reality such as heaven, and the spiritual realm in general is unknown.

Materialism: the most general term for belief that the material aspects of reality are all there is to reality. Materialists ascribe to materialism. The label of materialist (or related terms such as adherent to scientism or secular humanism) has no implication about the person's intelligence, level of education, morality, sanity, decency, or other attributes as a person. The only negative attached to any version of materialism comes from a lack of candor about the perspective if one falsely claims it is somehow scientific instead of merely being an assumption or belief.

Perspective: one dictionary definition of perspective is "evaluation of events according to a way of looking at them." That is exactly what perspective means in this book.

Physicalism: a term from philosophy, basically the same as materialism; physicalism assumes there is nothing beyond physical (material) aspects of reality.

Reality: reality is what is. Reality is complex and consists of material aspects, spiritual aspects, the two interact, and reality has infinite aspects.

Scientism: a subset of materialism that pertains to the arena of science.

Secular Humanism: basically ignores religious or spiritual aspects of reality, and bases values, morals, and ethics on a naturalistic perspective on material aspects of reality in the realms of human endeavor. A secular humanist is an adherent to the beliefs and practices of secular humanism. In the past century, secular humanism has come to dominate public education in America.

Soul: this word is ambiguous in this book. It has several different connotations depending upon the context in which it appears. Dictionaries have a variety of connotations for soul. One connotation is the immortal part of a person. A similar yet different connotation is the part of a person that is distinct from the person's body which led to numerous efforts to try to identify physical characteristics of the soul such as its weight. In the New Testament portion of Christian Scripture the word normally translated by soul is the Greek word from which we get psychology. The Scripture sometimes uses that word for the whole person (Acts 27:37). The Scripture uses that word for the part of a person different from the body of the person (Matthew 10:28). The Scripture uses that word for the part of the person different from the person's body or the person's spirit (1 Thessalonians 5:23). There is a part of a person that is directly related to God. The Scripture says human sin nature and sinful actions have killed that so the person is spiritually dead until the person is regenerated (made alive spiritually by the new/second birth). The state of that part of a person at physical death determines the person's eternal destiny (heaven for the ones with a living spiritual part, hell for the others). This is the immortal part of the person that dictionaries call the soul. It is the soul when a person is viewed as body and soul. But when a person is viewed as body, soul, and spirit; that part which determines a person's eternal destiny is the spirit and the soul then refers to the personality (intelligence, emotion, and will).

Spirit: in Scripture the spirit of a person normally refers to the part of the person that interacts with God. That is the way this term is used in this book. Sometimes the Scripture and Christians use the word Spirit to refer to the Holy Spirit, the Third Person of the Trinity. This book never uses the word "Spirit" alone to refer to the Holy Spirit except in quotations from Scripture where it is clear that the Holy Spirit is being referenced.

Spiritual aspects of reality: the spiritual aspects of reality begin with God because as Jesus told the Samaritan woman at the well, "God is Spirit" and He must be understood properly (i.e., "in truth") to worship Him (John 4:24). Hence anything related to God, even if it involves material aspects of reality in significant ways (such as parting of the Red Sea so a couple of million Jews with their animals and possessions could cross it on foot) is properly part of the spiritual aspects of reality or a manifestation of interactions of spiritual aspects of reality with its material aspects. In additions there a multitude of things largely outside what is generally considered to be the material aspects of reality that are in the spiritual aspects of reality; these include heaven, angels, demons, and the like. Also some aspect of people is spiritual and part of the spiritual aspects of reality. Unfortunately it is difficult to determine what the boundary (if there is a fixed boundary, there may not be one) between the spiritual aspects of a person and the material aspects of a person is. Therefore, the spiritual aspects of reality are fuzzy and not easily defined explicitly. Although the spiritual aspects of reality are often considered distinct from reality's material aspect, some of the spiritual aspects of reality are entwined with reality's material aspects.

Human capability to observe spiritual aspects of reality, whether by human senses or by technology, are limited. Hence, CCR assumes that reliable information about spiritual aspects of reality is best obtained from the Christian Scripture and contends that it should be the primary, perhaps the only reliable, source of information about the spiritual aspects of reality.

Theology: theology is basically the study of God; it is basically the collection of doctrines of a religious group (where doctrine refers to beliefs about a particular topic or point).

Truth: for CCR truth is correspondence with reality; that connotation transcends more limited definitions (such as compliance with a standard, such as finite reasoning/logic and observable evidence).

Uncertainty: dictionaries give a simple connotation for uncertainty: what is not known for certain. That connotation is exactly how uncertainty is used in this book IF the connotation for certainty stated above determines what is known for certain. Uncertainty, as stated above, is everything that is not a certainty.

Chapter 2.

MATERIAL ASPECTS OF REALITY

C CR'S APPROACH TO reality is dictated by the first three of CCR's six basic principles: 1) CCR addresses all of reality; 2) CCR applies the same honest and candid approach to all aspects of reality (this makes clear distinction between certainties and uncertainties); and 3) CCR recognizes the limitations of human perception (even with technological capabilities, such as sensors that permit detection of frequencies beyond those which a person can see, hear, or feel).

These basic CCR principles are fully compatible with the approach of modern science. The scientific approach has three basic elements: 1) collection of information about a topic that describes its characteristics and behavior; 2) development of mathematical formulae that describe such; and 3) collection of additional information about a topic to confirm the appropriateness of the mathematical formulae (or to modify and correct the formulae).

The history of science identifies two problems that continue to plague modern science. First, sometimes the information that mathematical formulae describing characteristics and behavior of something are based upon do not fully address that something's characteristics and behavior; or sometimes the formulae do not correctly represent all characteristics and behavior of the something accurately. This is particularly a problem when the formulae fail to fully address potential impact of all environmental factors such as velocities, pressure, temperature, radiation, etc. when those factors may be extreme. This is illustrated by the discovery a century ago of relativistic effects on mass and time as velocity approaches the speed of light. Second, sometimes the distinction between proven fact (a CCR certainty) and not-yet-falsified theory (a CCR uncertainty) is not clearly maintained in what is considered scientific "knowledge." For example, this happens when a proven fact (such as a "law" of behavior for something) is extrapolated to apply in environmental conditions for which confirming evidence of its appropriateness is limited or lacking.

Of course, science and religion share a common problem. They both involve people. Christianity has long realized that the primary problem of the church is the people in it. That too is the primary problem of science: the people who do it. For example, human desire for success (advancement, recognition, etc.) is a factor in exaggerated claims by scientists, in judicious selection of data to support an idea or theory, in such partisan support for an idea that other possibilities are rejected out of hand without due consideration, etc. CCR's emphasis on honesty and candor clearly distinguishing certainty from uncertainty (in both the spiritual and material aspects of reality) is a counter to the problem humans bring to both religion and science.

Reality has both material and spiritual aspects, and they can interact. Any perspective that does not address all of reality should be considered defective. Some of reality is not easily observed or understood; this is illustrated in the material aspects of reality by Dark Energy and Dark Matter which cannot be observed directly by current technology.

Suggestions about Dark Matter (or similar ideas) began to appear in the 18th and 19th centuries as efforts were made to explain the behavior of astronomical objects which was inconsistent with expectations based upon physics principles; suggestions about Dark Energy (or something similar) in terms of contemporary cosmology only began to appear in scientific literature a couple of decades ago.[7] At this time it is generally assumed by the scientific community that the major part of energy and matter in the universe are Dark Matter and Dark Energy.

CCR contends that spiritual aspects of reality as well as some of reality's material aspects are beyond capabilities of contemporary technology to observe directly although their impact can be seen at times on things that we can observe, but even what is observed may be beyond the capabilities of human explanation in regard to details of the mechanisms involved. As scientific knowledge and technology advance, mechanisms that previously had been beyond explanation by previous understanding sometimes become understandable. For this reason, this book usually indicates how long various levels of scientific knowledge have been available. This helps one to know when a particular explanation of things (such as geocentricism) became out of date. For example, most of the subatomic particles in the standard model of particle physics were discovered during the past century.

Dark Matter provides an example of such unobservable phenomena by contemporary technology in the material aspect of reality. The heavenly location of various spiritual items, such as the eternal destination of all whom Jesus saves, is an example of something not capable of direct observation by current technology in the spiritual aspect of reality. CCR classifies such as part of the spiritual aspects of reality, but recognizes that essentially nothing about the possible material attributes of such spiritual aspects of reality is known.

As noted previously in the section on terminology, this book has a very comprehensive connotation for the material aspects of reality. The material aspects of reality are anything consisting of atoms or subatomic particles (including point particles) — which this book calls matter (including the corresponding antimatter and all forces related to them). The total combination of such comprises the material aspect of reality. This is as expansive as one can get in defining the material aspects of reality. It includes things like photons and light (which are outside the definitions of matter for some) as well as forces like gravity and electromagnetic waves. It also is compatible with contemporary ideas that are undecided about how many dimensions the universe (or multiverse) may have.

Reality is so complex there is lack of agreement in the scientific community about reality's number of dimensions, and a question of whether reality is a universe or a multiverse. Consequently when one thinks of heaven as a place, there is ambiguity about its characteristics. Is it material in someway? Or only spiritual? This book will not solve such problems. CCR simply posits such is spiritual, but allows for the possibility that heaven may also have physical (material) attributes.

Jesus giving sight to a man born blind provides an example of interaction between the spiritual aspect of reality and the material aspect. CCR recognizes all of these aspects of reality. Not all perspectives on reality are as comprehensive as CCR. Some even make false claims of addressing all reality when actually just addressing part of reality.

The challenge of grappling with the complexities of reality and potential misunderstanding about reality as it is grappled with by CCR and others are not new. A classic example of confusion and misunderstanding from dealing with limited perception of reality comes from Plato's *Republic* (6th century B.C.) in Plato's Cave (sometimes called The Allegory of the Cave).[8] Plato deals with misconceptions based upon a limited exposure to reality, and misinterpretation of what happened to those freed from the cave bondage when they returned to the cave. Unfortunately attitudes of some materialists seem similar to that of those bound in the cave. They mistakenly take some of reality for its totality and make untrue comments about those who present a perspective contrary to their own.

The next section addresses certainties and uncertainties of the material aspects of reality. After that, comments are presented about materialistic perspectives that fail to give due regard to spiritual aspects of reality.

2.1. Certainties and Uncertainties in the Material Aspects of Reality

Certainties of the material aspects of reality are restricted to information based upon direct observation and associated measurement with extensive information about measurement conditions; everything else is uncertainties. This perspective is similar to the philosophy of science expressed by Sir Karl Popper who made a clear distinction between "proven" facts and simply "not yet falsified" theory (some call that approach "empirical falsification").

A great deal of scientific knowledge is based upon indirect observation. Many experiments in physics cannot directly observe what is being examined. In such a situation, assumptions are made about what will happen; then experimenters try to see if expected consequences occur. For example, if a particle collides with a particular item, certain observable products are expected. Such is an example of indirect observation (in contrast to direct observation). Indirect observation depends upon a number of assumptions, which is why CCR treats information from such experiments as uncertainty instead of certainty.

CCR normally puts "not yet falsified" elements of modern science in the uncertainty bin; but makes an exception for theories based upon extensive information from direct observation and associated measurement with known conditions. Thus, some theories that have not yet been falsified are considered in the certainty bin; these mainly are physical laws for how processes perform in a normal earth environment when applied in the contemporary normal earth environment.

Unfortunately this is an age of credulousness. Many people are prone to accept what comes out of computers as true and valid. They ignore the acronym GIGO from the early days of digital computers (the 1950s). GIGO stands for "garbage in, garbage out." If incorrect information goes into a computer, what comes out will also be incorrect. That has been forgotten or ignored by many, and prominence is given to what computers produce without due consideration to the quality of information used by the computer for its results.

Potential implications of such are very disturbing. For example, facial recognition processes by computers will not just be used to confirm identification of specific people (as is currently being done extensively by governmental authorities), but such computerized facial processing also will be used to characterize people. Humans know their visual impressions of a person are not completely accurate all the time, and sensible people use additional observation and interactions with the person to confirm or modify their initial assessment of the person based upon appearance. When a computer classifies a person as gay or straight based upon his or her image (currently computers do that better than people based upon just looking at images of the person; in testing computer capability for such classification, computers were correct more than 70% of the time based upon analysis of an image of a person), that information goes into a file someplace and may impact decisions about the person's suitability for a loan, a job, or something else. However such computer systems may not have been programmed to have the human wisdom of reserving final judgment until adequate information about the person has been obtained to make a final decision about the initial assessment based upon processing an image. It is most likely that the person will be impacted by whatever the computer initially put into the file about that person. Such credulousness as the trust given to computer results also impacts people's perspectives on reality; that is something that CCR can help to correct.

"Direct observation" means the item itself is observed, not observation of a by-product from the item's interactions with other things. It also means that all pertinent factors of the relationship between the object, the observer, and the measurement instrumentation are fully specified since such can impact the observation and measurement in some situations. This restriction moves much of knowledge claimed by modern science from the certainty category to the uncertainty category (where it belongs since it is based so much on assumptions rather than direct observation). For example, modern science states what it believes temperature to be inside the fireball of a nuclear explosion and inside stars. No contemporary instrument can measure such directly or survive in such an environment. Hence the predicted temperatures that science "believes" for such are not based upon direct observation. Classifying something about the material aspect of reality as an uncertainty does not mean it is wrong or not supported by substantial evidence; it merely means it is not "proven" in the Popper sense. Instead of being a fact, it is just a "not yet falsified hypothesis."

Liquid water illustrates why direct observation is essential for certainty. The density of liquid H_2O (water) changes with temperature. Most of the time, density decreases as temperature increases. Hence some would think that a theory that described that density decrease for liquid H_2O should be treated as a certainty; but water does not always increase in volume as temperature increases for the full temperature range of H_2O's liquid state. For four degrees Centigrade before water changes from liquid to solid (ice), the density of liquid H_2O (water) decreases as temperature decreases.[9] This illustrates the value of the perspective that only direct observation provides certain information. Full description of the behavior of liquid H_2O (water) based upon observation with appropriate documentation of observation conditions is accepted as a certainty for situations with a typical environment of earth conditions relative to gravitational, pressure, and radiation forces.

"Not yet falsified" theory may work much or even most of the time, but a certainty in the material aspect of reality is restricted to things that work ALL the time. Well attested laws of biology, chemistry, and physics usually work currently in the normal earth environment (i.e., one experiencing the usual levels of gravitational force, pressure, and radiation at speeds well away from the speed of light) and for such is considered a certainty; but the assumption that such laws have always worked (or will always work) that way on earth or elsewhere is an uncertainty. It is easy to see why CCR considers such an uncertainty. It was only a century ago that Einstein suggested that both time and mass can be impacted by speed when speed approaches the speed of light.[10]

That association with the situation's conditions had previously been unrecognized. It is common practice for science to fail to comprehensively identify all conditions pertinent to a stated functionality. Many outside (and some within) scientific and technical communities are not aware of how common (frequent) this problem is. Numerous studies in recent years have criticized respected peer-reviewed scientific publications (usually considered the pinnacle of authoritative information) for drawing invalid conclusions frequently (up to about 30% of the situations assessed) from statistics used because of failure to appropriately identify sources and conditions of data analyzed and for using inappropriate statistical processes.

Assumptions about universality of the laws of biology, chemistry, and physics noted above are based upon absence of situation dependencies such as noted for time and mass in the theory of relativity. There is no scientific basis for such assumptions; they merely show the prejudice of human arrogance which is reluctant to admit its limitations.

Lack of certainty in many areas of science does not prevent many useful things being done technically because most of the immediate applications of scientific theories occur within the context of situations where their guidance applies. However, when things are called "scientific" that apply those theories elsewhere (such as the past or outside our solar system), those theories may not provide reliable information. It would be much more honest to label such for what it is: speculation (not scientifically proven fact). Even when supported extensively by mathematics and observations thought to be related, it is still speculation (not scientific fact as it is frequently and wrongly presented to be).

It helps to remember how limited human direct observation of things and their measurement with relatively comprehensive awareness of situation circumstances actually is. Every bit of human direct observation comes from the few thousand years of human reported observations (which at most is something less than 0.01% of the estimated life thus far of matter, which current theory says expanded from a tiny speck at the Big Bang – this maximum of less than 0.01% of time assumes human observations go back a hundred thousand years: actual records other than a few cave drawings are from just a tenth of that length of time). Every human related observation occurred within our solar system, which is thought to occupy essentially zero percent of the observable universe. According to contemporary astronomy the sun in our solar system is one of hundreds of billions of stars in the Milky Way, our galaxy, which is one of more than a hundred billion galaxies in the observable universe. Assuming that what has been observed in this speck of space and time applies universally is an audacious speculation, and should be recognized as such. Assumption that such theories apply everywhere is acceptable scientifically, but presentation of them as proven to apply or stated that they have to apply is unacceptable. The assumption that such theories apply everywhere is no greater than other assumptions of current scientists. For example, some theories circulated among modern scientists assume the possibility of new space and time, and there are differences in the number of dimensions for reality from different theories currently in vogue.

Matter is normally said to exist in one of four or five states on earth (solid, liquid, gas, or plasma according to most; some add the Bose-Einstein condensates, a state of matter which exists only at temperatures very close to absolute zero). Another dozen states have been defined (sometimes they are called "exotic" states of matter) and are thought to exist in extreme conditions of temperature and pressure (some have been observed directly or nearly directly, such as superconductivity at or near absolute zero temperature, but other exotic states are only speculation, such as degenerate matter in white dwarf and neutron stars). This illustrates how limited the facts (i.e., certainties) of science are. Most of what is considered scientific knowledge today falls into the uncertainty bin because such is actually "not yet falsified" theory. This is why the current theory of how the universe spread from a tiny speck to what is observed today violates known or classical physical laws (its period of inflation[11]) and why widely accepted descriptions of how things are (the Standard Model of particle physics, Theory of Relativity, and quantum physics) have various incompatibilities.[12]

Too many, either explicitly or implicitly, take the perspective of materialism and physicalism that there is nothing but the material and physical in reality; that perspective assumes that in time science will be able to explain everything. It is always refreshing to see recognition that such is not the case. In his 2016 book (*The Physics of Time*), experimental physicist Richard A. Muller[13] notes that physics has limitations; it is incomplete and "never will be capable of describing all of reality." (p. 10)

The purpose of this discussion of uncertainties in the material aspect of reality is not to disparage the marvelous technical accomplishments of modern science (for there are many); instead it is to demonstrate the foolishness of those who claim that the material aspect of reality is all there is. How could such a claim be thought credible by any thinking person who is aware of the uncertainties of the material world? What could be a factual or logical basis for such a claim? It cannot be based on valid scientific methodology. Denying the existence of the spiritual aspect of reality merely reflects prejudices and assumptions of those making such a claim.

2.2. Unscientific and Irrational Behavior of Some Materialists

"Materialist" is used simply as a description of someone who assumes that the materialistic aspect of reality is all there is; nothing else interacts with the material aspects of reality ("physicalism" is a term with basically the same meaning as "materialism;" physicalism entered the terminology of philosophy in the 1930s). The term "materialist" in this book does not imply anything about the person's intelligence, education, emotional maturity, ethics, or values. The term simply means the person does not believe there is a spiritual (non-material) aspect to reality. Sometimes other terms are used of materialists in particular areas, such as "scientism" for application of materialism in the scientific arena, especially in areas of biology, chemistry, and physics. Likewise secular humanism has been used for application of materialism in the humanities.

Some materialists are atheists. Honest ones will admit their atheism is a belief, not a scientific position. Some contend that atheism, secular humanism, etc. are religions without the formal organizational structure associated with religious groups. Others deny such classification as a religion. The point is moot. Whether or not such things should be called a religion does not change the point made here: such ideas are belief. The ideas of materialism are assumption based; they are not an established scientific fact based upon direct observation and measurement with comprehensive statement of pertinent conditions.

Assertion that a particular belief (such as atheism) is "scientific" is contrary to basic scientific principles. It is very hard to prove that something cannot be. To say something does not exist because one has not seen or detected that something is not proof unless one can claim to have a detection device that can detect everything and one has looked everywhere. Certainly no one alive today can validly make such a claim since it is generally acknowledged that the majority of the mass and energy in the universe which we can observe parts of is outside the capabilities of current technology to observe directly; and sane people are intelligent enough not to think that even if a device were to exist that could detect Dark Matter and Dark Energy it would not prove that everything which existed could be detected.

It is dishonest and unethical for atheists to claim a "scientific" basis for their atheism; and it is shameful for other scientists not to criticize such a claim as unscientific. Both those making false claims of a scientific basis for atheism and those being quiet about the phoniness of the "science" aspect of the claim have lousy ethics. Perhaps they are only "mistaken" instead of being unethical because they have a different connotation for "science" than its usual connotation. While a person has a right to be an atheist or to believe in atheism, that right does not include the right to falsely claim such a belief is a scientific conclusion from actual evidence. It is important to respect the right of a person to believe whatever he or she chooses to believe, even if the person's beliefs are silly (such as the beliefs of those who are sincere in the International Flat Earth Society).[14]

It is also important to warn people of potential consequences from their beliefs. Most people would consider it appropriate to warn someone whose retirement plan is to win the lottery that it is most likely that he or she will be destitute. Likewise most people would consider it appropriate to tell someone who is unconcerned about eating healthfully that he or she is likely to experience unnecessary medical problems. However, some of those who consider the two previous examples appropriate would consider it inappropriate to tell a person who chooses not to turn to Jesus for eternal salvation that they will not like their situation after death. It is interesting that people who would not criticize someone for warning a person about the dangers of a lottery-system retirement plan or about the dangers of unhealthy eating are offended when a person offers a similar warning in the spiritual realm; some people have amazing double standards.

Materialists who are not atheists reject God's current involvement in the universe even if they posit the possibility that God created the universe (but then left it and no longer has any involvement with it). However, it is clear that many in science are not materialists, but have belief in God. This is illustrated by Tihomir Dimitrov's free e-book (developed 1995-2008) *50 Nobel Laureates and Other Great Scientists Who Believe in God* (http://nobelist.tripod.com/sitebuildercontent/sitebuilderfiles/50-no-belists.pdf accessed October 2017). Zeeya Merali's book (*A Big Bang in a Little Room: The Quest To Create New Universes*, Basic Books, 2017) presents religious views of scientists at the forefront of physics and cosmology as she describes the state of that part of science (i.e., physics and cosmology).

Most materialists have no widely accepted explanation for creation (how something came into existence from nothing, although some say various mathematics used in cosmology implies something can come from nothing) and many (perhaps most of them) do not believe that matter and energy are eternal. Christians and others believing in God have an answer: God created what exists; and they recognize that their belief is a matter of faith, not scientific fact. Christian Scripture is clear about that perspective: faith is required to recognize and relate properly to God (Hebrews 11:1-3 & 6).

Some materialists deny the possibility of miracles; others simply consider miracles to be events that cannot yet be explained by material processes and expect that future scientific advances will bring appropriate explanations for the "miraculous" events. In contrast, CCR believes miracles are possible and even can suggest a mechanism for them that might appeal to those with a scientific bent. Think of a miracle as an insertion of matter or energy into a situation by God. Compared to the amount of matter and energy God used in creation, even a major miracle from a physical perspective (such as dividing the Red Sea for Moses and the Israelites to cross, the total involved a couple of million people plus animals and possessions) is only a flick of an eyelash compared to creation. This is an assumption as to how a miracle may occur; there are other possible explanations.

Materialists who deny the Creator and the possibility of miracles appear to lack scientific integrity if they are not explicit and clear that their position is based upon their beliefs and assumptions; it is not something based upon the certainty of proven scientific evidence. False claims or exaggerated claims are a bane scientifically, but they occur relatively frequently. For example, "exaggerated results in peer-reviewed scientific studies have reached epidemic proportions in recent years," John P. A. Ioannidis, "An Epidemic of False Claims," *Scientific American*, June 1, 2011. The problem of exaggeration from scientists is continuing and may even be getting worse.

Because CCR approaches all of reality the same way, dealing with both material and spiritual aspects of reality with honesty and candor about what is certain and what is uncertain, it is hoped that those immersed within secular humanism will be encouraged to re-examine their perspective and approach it with the same kind of honesty and candor that CCR manifests. If that happens, some immersed in secular humanism may discover that some of their precepts are deceptive and not consistent with reality. Possibly such realization will lead them to reconsider the spiritual aspects of reality. If that happens, it will be very beneficial both for the individuals involved and for our society. Everyone benefits when total reality is dealt honestly with candor.

The world has far too many instances of the negative consequences of forced acceptance of views by those dominant politically; honest and candid dealing with reality is always better for the people of a society. Decent people who are immersed within secular humanism should be ashamed of the deceptive way it treats part of reality as the whole of reality. Of course, die-hards and most partisans are not concerned much with reality; they only care about maintaining the perspective they endorse.

Chapter 3.

SPIRITUAL ASPECTS OF REALITY

R EALITY IS INFINITE and complex. It contains both spiritual and material aspects which interact. The fact that we cannot observe spiritual things directly in most situations further complicates things, especially when we discuss the spiritual aspects of reality. That limitation in human perception (the third CCR principle) and its implications are discussed here briefly before turning to general discussion of the spiritual aspects of reality.

Since limitations in human perception preclude direct observation of spiritual aspects of reality and their measurement with full explication of measurement factors, CCR cannot consider any spiritual aspect of reality as a certainty. Hence all spiritual aspects of reality are uncertainties. Every spiritual aspect of reality has to be approached by faith, i.e., with assumptions that provide the basis for what is presented as information about those spiritual aspects of reality. Thus, information about spiritual aspects of reality is what Popper would call "not-yet-falsified" theory. There may be abundant evidence in support of such, but it is not fact proven by direct observation and adequate explication of the measurement and the measurement process.

This perspective will probably upset some who are prone to make statements of extreme certainty about God and spiritual things; but it is an honest and candid facing of reality. It also should embarrass much of the modern scientific and educational establishment by comparison since they so often fail to employ similar honesty and candor in their domains.

Since God existed before anything He created and He is spiritual, spiritual aspects of reality existed before the material aspects of reality. The Scripture does not tell about the beginning of spiritual aspects of reality other than God, but there is a hint that at least some spiritual aspects of reality besides God existed before some material aspects of reality. For example Job 38:4-7 indicates spiritual beings (sons of God, angels) as well as the morning stars existed when God made the earth. For topics addressed in this book, it does not matter whether or not any spiritual aspect of reality other than God existed before the material aspects of reality. The point is mentioned here merely to illustrate that CCR is considering all aspects of reality (its first principle).

3.1. Limitations in Human Perception Make Spiritual Aspects of Reality Uncertain

A key aspect of the spiritual aspects of reality, at least from the human perspective, is people; therefore, it is appropriate to consider the nature of people since they have both physical and spiritual aspects. Christian Scripture (the only kind of material referenced in this book as "Scripture" and which generally includes material contained in the Hebrew Bible as well as the New Testament), which CCR considers the primary general source of reliable information about spiritual aspects of reality, presents a variety of views about people.

Although it is clear that people have both spiritual and material aspects, Scripture sometimes refers to people as a whole, without making distinction between their spiritual and material aspects. At times, just a part of the person refers to the whole person. This illustrated by Acts 27:37 where Luke says there were 276 "souls" on board the ship in a storm. Whole people were on board; not just the non-material aspect of them. Many modern translations hide that by translating the Greek word for "soul" by "person" or another term for whole human. Other times Scripture refers to people as having two parts (one material and the other non-material). This is illustrated by Jesus' warning to be more concerned about the One (God) Who can destroy both "soul and body" in hell than to fear those who can only kill the body (Matthew 10:28). And sometimes the Scripture refers to people as having three parts: body, soul, and spirit (1 Thessalonians 5:23).

How the material and non-material aspects of a person interact is complicated and not always clear or obvious. Materialists would deny existence of the spiritual aspect of a person and posit that the mental and emotional aspects of a person (which appear to be non-material) are caused by the way the person's brain is functioning. Christian Scripture has a different perspective, as noted above.

When the three-part (tripartite) perspective of a person is used, the body refers to the obvious material reality of the person. The soul addresses the personality: intellect, emotions, and will (volition); this aspect of the person sometimes appears to be non-material and at other times it seems to be capable of reasonably full explanation by functioning of the person's brain. The spirit refers to the part of the person that interacts with God. Scripture says that the spirit is dead (a consequence of a person's sin nature) until a person is born-again through faith in Jesus as Savior (Ephesians 2:1-10 addresses this specifically, as does the Apostle Paul's full explanation of God's plan of salvation in Romans). When a two-part perspective on the person is presented (body and soul), the soul includes both the "soul" (i.e., the personality: intellect, emotion, and will) and "spirit" (the connection with God).

Interactions among the three parts of the person are imperfectly and only partially understood. With the advances in technology that allow levels of observation of the human physically never before possible (by CAT, MRI, and other means), modern neuroscience[15] has dramatically increased our comprehension of how brain functioning impacts aspects of the personality. Such has raised challenges to the theological concept of "free will."[16] If one's personality is just the product of how one's brain functions, what happens to responsibility for one's choices and actions when one's normal brain functioning is interfered with by illness or injury?

This issue (free will or responsibility) is showing up in a variety of arenas, not just in medicine and religion. For example, new terms are beginning to show up in legal arenas. One is "neurocriminality" (defined as "a neural basis to crime") used in the context of those committing violent crime repetitively.[17] There's also a relatively new discipline called "neurolaw" (a term coined by Sherrod Taylor in 1991 as "an emerging field of interdisciplinary study that explores effects of discoveries in neuroscience on legal rules and standards").

Why is this important? It's important because responsibility depends upon choice. If a person has no choice, is that person responsible for consequences of the choice? If an important paper is mistakenly put in a shredder and the paper is destroyed, the machine should not be blamed for doing what it was designed to do (if it performed properly). The shredder has no responsibility for the mistake in destroying an important paper. Responsibility for that lies elsewhere.

Christian Scripture is clear: God holds people responsible for evil choices they make. This is clearly stated by the Apostle Paul in Romans 1: 18-32 (as well as in many other passages). However, it is also clear that some people have less capacity for making a proper choice than others. Young children do not have the same capability for proper choice as adults do. Those with severe mental limitations and various medical conditions have limited choice; for example, a person in an epileptic seizure (some people call such a seizure a "fit") may damage and break things without consciously choosing to do so.

Modern technology has enabled brain scans to detect abnormalities (such as tumors) in brains of some convicted of multiple violent crimes. When the tumor was removed in one case, the person no longer behaved with the previous characteristic violence. The person behaved decently for years; then the violence returned as the tumor returned. When the tumor was removed again, the violent behavior also went away.[18] In a situation such as this, should the person be held responsible for the violent behavior when it was evidently caused by the tumor in the brain that changed the way the person thought and acted?

Direct observations of the inner workings of the human brain are recent; X-rays of the brain were first done about a century ago, and computerized axial tomography (CAT or CT scanning) and magnetic resonance imaging (MRI) began less than half a century ago. A great deal of progress has been made in gaining knowledge about normal functioning of the human brain, but there is substantial evidence that the brain operates differently in some people at some times. With over 80 billion neutrons in the human brain, each of which can have thousands of connections (synapses) with other neutrons, there are a very large number of alternative ways information (signals) can pass around the brain. It is known that sometimes when there has been physical injury to the brain (or surgical action) that the brain creates new pathways for signals when the original normal pathway is no longer possible.

Current medical science understands how certain situations can have a major impact on a person's thinking and behavior (as it did with the man guilty of repeated violence with brain tumor mentioned earlier), but medical science has not shown that such brain situations always produce such thinking or behavior in a significant number of people. Hence the tendency to dismiss free will and say a person is simply a product of the way the brain functions in the situation, which some who reject spiritual realities have said, is quite unjustified by the present state of knowledge.

Claims of scientific knowledge at times go far beyond what the evidence supports. A classic instance of such is the false claim that finger prints are sufficiently unique that they provide unequivocal evidence of a person's identity. Generally fingerprints provide a useful guide to identification of a person; but fingerprint identification is not always correct. Numerous articles about wrongful convictions based upon fingerprint evidence exist.[19] Although fingerprints have been used by police, in court, and at borders for the past century, solid scientific evidence specifying their error rate is hard to find. For some reason, the courts seem unwilling to apply the Daubert criteria required of other scientific evidence presented in court.[20] Fingerprint witnesses in court sometimes present claims of fingerprint accuracy for their conclusions that are not real.[21] The literature about free will from those involved with neuroscience sometimes has the same flavor as erroneously excessive claims for fingerprint uniqueness.

The CCR view on this complex subject of free will and responsibility in light of brain malfunctioning is clear: Scripture tells us that God holds people accountable for their decisions and actions; but how God will evaluate those with limited mental capabilities, such as young children, those with brain injuries or disease, or those whose biology significantly hinders normal brain processes is not known. Whatever God does will be right, just, and based upon full knowledge of everything related to the situation. It will be the appropriate judgment, regardless of how people may look at it.

The end of the first chapter of Job provides a good example of the attitude all should have about God's actions. The following is Job's response to learning that all of his children had been killed by a storm. Job 1:20-22. "[20] Then Job arose and tore his robe and shaved his head and fell on the ground and worshiped. [21] And he said, 'Naked I came from my mother's womb, and naked shall I return. The Lord gave, and the Lord has taken away; blessed be the name of the Lord.' [22] In all this Job did not sin or charge God with wrong." (ESV)

Human arrogance is something that God does not appreciate. That is demonstrated in God's response to the Tower of Babel (Genesis 11:1-8) as well as in Paul's comments in Romans 1:18-32. Human arrogance shows in human foolishness of trying to live without God and in people's criticism of how God works and what He does. Perhaps thinking about advances in medical science and the questions such raise about free will stimulate some to seek to better understand God and how He acts, and cause them not to be so presumptuous as to criticize Him or advise Him about how things should be done. The limitations of our finite reasoning and human incomplete awareness of things needs to be recognized. Such should encourage appreciation for God's mercy and grace in providing a way for people to have a proper relationship with Him through His Son, Jesus Christ the Savior.

People seldom think carefully about the substance of a person. The above discussion illustrates how little is understood about the spiritual aspects of people; likewise people fail to think very deeply about the material aspects of people. They only think about things at macro levels. A common estimate of the number of atoms in a person's body is 7×10^{27}; that is a very big number. Many are more impressed when they realize that a large number of atoms in a person's body are changing constantly. All atoms in some parts, such as skin or the liver, are totally changed (i.e., replaced) in a matter of weeks; others, such as the heart, may take months to be changed. It is thought that all the atoms in a person are changed in some small number of years (five years is one of the common estimates). Everyone's body contains atoms that once were in someone else's body. If a person is in a room or a vehicle with other people for any length of time, at least some atoms that were breathed out by another person have been breathed in by that person and have gone into that person's body.

It is sobering to realize how little there is of a person. Atoms are mainly empty space. If all the empty spaces were taken away and just the solid stuff was left, it would take all the stuff from millions of people for a cubic centimeter of stuff. That's a cube just half-an-inch on each side! Some estimate that all the solid stuff from the billions of people on the planet today could be contained in less than one cubic foot!

This is mentioned here in discussion of spiritual aspects of reality because so little is understood about the spiritual aspects of reality. It is important to remember also that far less about the material aspects of reality is understood than many presume to be the case. These simple comments about some aspects of the material aspects of reality emphasize similar limitations in understanding spiritual aspects of reality.

3.2. Christian Scripture: The Basis for Belief about Spiritual Aspects of Reality

God has revealed Himself and provided information to people in a variety of ways. He spoke as a voice from heaven. He appeared in human form a few times in the Old Testament and in the person of Jesus of Nazareth. He communicated through agents (such as the angel Gabriel and various prophets) and through unusual items such as a burning bush. He communicated with people through dreams and visions. He also communicated in writing (directly in the tablets given to Moses and indirectly through the inspired writings by people that comprise Christian Scripture). Of these various communications from God, CCR believes that the one which provides the most reliable general guidance for people in general (not just for the ones who received it initially) is Christian Scripture (this is CCR's fourth principle).

Some present reasons to accept the Scripture as authoritative beyond comments about such from the Scripture itself. CCR does not do that; instead CCR follows the example of many noted Christians who attest that the Scripture authenticates itself. Few have stated this point as eloquently as John Calvin in his *Institutes of the Christian Religion* (I.vii.1, 2, 5) where he says:

"illumined by His power, we believe neither by our own nor by anyone else's judgment that Scripture is from God; but above human judgment we affirm with utter certainty (just as if we were gazing upon the majesty of God Himself) that it has flowed to us from the very mouth of God by the ministry of men. We seek no proofs, no marks of genuineness upon which our judgment may lean; but we subject our judgment and wit to it as to a thing far beyond any guesswork!"[22]

Formal statements of belief by different Christian groups often mention Scripture as a basis for their theology and as a reliable guide to people regarding how to live. Sometimes the writings considered Scripture are named explicitly. Generally Scripture is said to have been produced under the inspiration of God the Holy Spirit. "Verbal" and "plenary" are terms sometimes used to describe Scriptural inspiration, meaning that the very words used were the ones that God intended and that everything in the Scripture is what God intended. Some include a statement about Biblical inerrancy.[23]

Normally such formal statements of belief about the Scripture say that characteristics ascribed to Scripture (such as "verbal" and "plenary") apply specifically to the autographs (the original manuscripts of the portions of Scripture). Sometimes comments are made about the relation to the autographs of extant copies of those materials and the versions of the Scripture used by people today; but often that critical subject is left unaddressed and when comments are made about it they reflect more a hope that what is available today is an acceptably accurate representation of the original Scriptural material than an expression of actual reality supported by specific evidence.

The Scripture itself does not explicitly identify what writings are Scripture in more detail than Jesus' words about "the law of Moses, the prophets, and the Psalms" (Luke 24:44); the Scripture says nothing about the accuracy of later copies of the original manuscripts of the Scripture. Consequently there are uncertainties about which writings are Scripture, exactly what those writings say, and how such should be interpreted. These uncertainties are addressed in the context of the perceptions of the early church. Belief and practice of the early church (a time before social privilege and political acceptance corrupted Christian ideas as much as occurred later, and a time when Christian writers were just a few generations from the original apostles of Jesus and writers of the New Testament) provide a useful guide for addressing the issues that this book considers.

Spiritual aspects of reality are difficult to observe. Some spiritual aspects of reality (such as the Creator's power and intelligence) can be deduced from our observation of nature, as the Apostle Paul notes in Romans 1, but most of spiritual reality is outside human capability to observe directly. Theophanies, encounters with God or spiritual beings such as angels in a physical form (whether in human form or something else like the burning bush that Moses encountered), can be very impressive for those who encounter them but usually reveal little about the nature of the spiritual being and are subject to misinterpretation by the individuals involved. The same is also true for revelations from God by dreams and visions. Something more reliable is needed. These comments are based upon the second and third CCR principles (that CCR approaches all of reality with honesty and candor, recognizing limitations of human perception).

God has provided Christian Scripture as a reliable guide to spiritual aspects of reality for basically all people of all time. This is a primary assumption, presupposition, faith, etc. upon which CCR is based. This premise (the fourth CCR principle) is presented without justification here. Various books present the case for believing that Christian Scripture is reliable information from God. This book simply posits that such is the case, and leaves rationale for such to others.

There are three basic uncertainties associated with Christian Scripture: 1) which writings (books) should be considered Scripture, 2) what is the exact text of books considered Scripture (in essence, how does what exists today relate to what was written originally), and 3) what is the proper interpretation of Scripture passages. Each of these uncertainties is discussed in the following materials.

A fourth kind of uncertainty pertains to beliefs based upon the Scripture: the difficulty of describing correctly in finite language things related to the infinite. This is also addressed; it reflects the first CCR principle (which assumes that reality is complex with infinite aspects).

Uncertainties associated with Christian Scripture do not prevent confidence in truth from them. Such confidence can come from undisputed portions of Scripture where those truths are taught clearly in multiple passages. Such truth "certainties" provide the foundation of CCR beliefs (the fifth CCR principle). Key CCR tenets are based upon clear teachings from multiple passages of Scripture in undisputed sections of Scripture. Discussion of what "undisputed sections of Scripture" means and which Scripture are undisputed is addressed early in Chapter 4.

In addressing these uncertainties about Scripture, how Scripture was addressed in the early church is presented since that was an era when God was working powerfully through the church. That makes such an important consideration because some in the 20th century who emphasize the importance of Scriptural inspiration (and associated doctrines such as Biblical inerrancy) have indicated that without a strong emphasis on such an exalted view of Scripture, God is not likely to work powerfully through the church. Comments in this book do not fit neatly in that pigeon-hole; some may find what is presented here to be disturbing.

3.2.1. Which Books Are Scripture?

There are two basic approaches to determining which writings (books) are Christian Scripture. The way most people address this issue is simply to accept the tradition of the variety of Christianity to which they belong.

For Protestant Christians, that tradition began in the 16th century. For Catholic and Orthodox Christians, their traditions were initiated about the 4th century (drawing upon some traditions that existed from earlier). For other varieties within Christendom, their traditions about Scripture go back to about the same era for when they began as they do for Catholics and the Orthodox. Traditions of Scripture for modern religious varieties within Christendom usually start when that religious variety began.

The tradition about the Jewish Bible (the Hebrew Tanak/Tanakh) probably began with the Masoretes (sixth to tenth centuries A.D.) who produced the Masoretic Text of the Hebrew Bible, although many would claim an earlier origin for the Jewish Bible. However, its content earlier may not been identical with that in the Tanak since the Septuagint (LXX, a Greek translation of the Hebrew Scripture about two centuries before Christ) contains additional books that are not in the Tanak and has different readings than the Masoretic Text in some passages. The LXX seems to have been accepted by at least some Jews in Judea as well as by Jews in the Diaspora during the first century.

The other approach for determining which writings are Scripture is to examine the historical evidence related to the writings and their acceptance by Christians as Scripture. This is an approach taken by most scholars, but generally those scholars are reluctant to rock the boat of tradition in their variety of Christianity by suggesting the tradition may not be consistent with the historical evidence. The reason for that is simple: it can cost a scholar who does that a lot. Some are not willing to risk possible loss of position and prestige.

In keeping with its second principle (addresses all aspects of reality with honesty and candor), CCR takes the historical evidence approach to determining which books are Scripture. Doing this focuses on the perspective of the early church about Scripture as well as on the historical evidence. This provides context for the perspective presented in this book. The early church (which ends about 240 A.D.) is an era during which Christian belief and practice had not been as corrupted by social privilege and political acceptance as shown by later church history. This allows the early church to be a more reliable guide in some ways than the church in other eras.

Nowhere in Christian Scripture is there a comprehensive list of writings that are Scripture. The Old Testament mentions both materials that are included in Christian Scripture (such as reference to the Chronicles of the kings of Israel and Judah in 1 Kings 14:19, 29) and materials (such as the book of Jasher in Joshua 10:13 or writings of the prophet Iddo in 2 Chronicles 9:29; 12:15; and 13:22) that are not included in Christian Scripture and are no longer extant.[24] The New Testament only has a general threefold description of the Old Testament by Jesus: "the Law of Moses and the Prophets and the Psalms" (Luke 24:44 ESV). The New Testament mentions Moses, David, Isaiah, Jeremiah, Daniel, Joel and Hosea in quoting the Old Testament. There is no more specific list in the New Testament of what writings were included in Old Testament Scripture than indicated by these comments.

Christian Scripture has two fundamental parts: the Old Testament and the New Testament. They are treated separately in the material below. Discussion of the canon of the Old Testament is presented first. The word "canon" is used for writings accepted as Scripture.

3.2.1.1. Canon of the Old Testament

There are mixed indications about what was considered Scripture by Jews in Judea and Galilee during the time of Christ's public ministry. There is nothing more definitive in Scripture itself than the three fold division of the Old Testament mentioned by Jesus and the quotations noted as Scripture by New Testament writers.

As an example of Jewish belief in that era, a first century Jewish historian, Josephus, makes reference to 22 books in Jewish Scripture but does not name them although he presents them in three categories: law (5), prophets (13), and hymns/rules for living (4).[25] The Jewish encyclopedia discussion of *Bible Canon* uses the 24 book arrangement of the Jewish Bible based upon Talmudic tradition represented by the Masoretic Text and mentions controversy about canonicity of some books in that tradition from the time of Christ and a century or two earlier.[26] The LXX is a translation that included all of the books of the Hebrew Bible plus others. Most of the LXX was translated before 200 B.C. and may represent better readings of the Hebrew Bible in some passages because of Jewish problems in the first half of the second century B.C.[27] The New Testament, though written mainly by Jews from Galilee and Paul who had been formally trained in Jerusalem although he was from Tarsus (in modern Turkey), usually quotes from the LXX when it differs from the Masoretic Text. It is also noteworthy that Josephus (a first century Jew in the land of the Jews) used the LXX in some of his writing. These facts suggest that during the first century some Jews in the Holy Land considered the LXX as Scripture just as Jews in the Diaspora did. Jewish rejection of the LXX did not become widespread until a century or two after the Romans destroyed Jerusalem. That rejection of the Greek version of the Hebrew Bible by Jews and emphasis only on the Hebrew version was part of Jewish efforts to maintain a cultural identity.

The Hebrew Bible organizes its material differently than the way material is organized in Christian Old Testaments; but generally what is contained in the Hebrew Bible (as represented by the Masoretic Text) is basically that which is contained in the Protestant Old Testament (i.e., the material does not include the *Apocrypha*). It is important to remember that in the first century the books of Scripture mainly were on separate scrolls (sometimes a scroll would contain several books, such as the five books of Moses in the Torah). Christian Scripture in the early church was not as a single item containing the entire Old Testament (or the entire New Testament) as is done with a modern version of the Bible. A codex (i.e., book like format) containing most of the Scripture or a large portion of it did not come into common use until a couple of centuries after Jesus was on the earth, late in the early church (or even after 240 A.D.).

Specification of the Masoretic Text as the Hebrew Scripture probably occurred centuries later than when Jesus was on the earth as a man. Once it was thought the Old Testament canon was established by Jewish rabbis about 90 A.D. at the Council of Jamnia (an idea first originated in the 19th century by Heinrich Graetz); that idea has been discredited. Details about establishment of the Old Testament canon are currently unknown; probably canonization occurred after the third or fourth century and before the 9th or 10th century (date of the oldest copy of the Masoretic Text outside Hebrew materials contained in the Dead Sea Scrolls).

Relative to whether or not the *Apocrypha* should be considered Scripture, some make much of the fact that none of the New Testament writers (except possibly Jude) quote anything from the *Apocrypha*. However, about half a dozen of the 39 books in the Protestant Old Testament are not quoted or referenced in any way by the New Testament; does not that make their status as Scripture also suspect as the silence about the *Apocrypha* is claimed to do by some?

It is unclear if the Essenes (a first century Jewish sect) viewed books from the *Apocrypha* found among the Dead Sea Scrolls differently than they viewed books of the Masoretic Text. In general, the early church seems to have taken the Old Testament of the LXX as its Old Testament Scripture. In the early church, some (e.g., Irenaeus) presumed that the Septuagint was translated by Jews before the era of Christ and that the Septuagint at certain places gave a more Christological interpretation than 2nd century Hebrew texts; this was taken as evidence that "Jews" had changed the Hebrew text in a way that made the text less Christological.

The bottom line about the Old Testament canon: there were uncertainties about it in the early church and there even seem to have been some uncertainties about it among Jews in Judea during the first century B.C. and the first century A.D.

3.2.1.2. Canon of the New Testament

Perhaps a good synopsis of the early church's perceptions regarding the canonicity of different materials can be found in the *Ecclesiastical History* by Eusebius (which was written about 325 A.D. less than a century after the end of the early church about 240 A.D.). Eusebius was leader (bishop) of Christians in Caesarea, the center of Christian learning and scholarship at the time. In the generation previous to that of Eusebius, Caesarea had been the primary location of Origen (perhaps the most famous Christian scholar of the third century) for two decades before his death and the center of his activities. Eusebius did not address the canon of Old Testament material. Relative to the New Testament, he categorizes possible Scripture in four categories: 1) as recognized (those in the 27 of the New Testament books not listed as disputed or spurious), 2) disputed (James, Jude, 2nd Peter, 2nd & 3rd John), 3) spurious (several books that some in the early church considered Scripture in addition to the 27 books currently in the New Testament, Eusebius said some considered Hebrews to be spurious, and Eusebius listed Revelation in both the recognized category and in the spurious category), or 4) heretical.[28]

It is important to be clear about a point that often does not get discussed when the canon of Christian Scripture is addressed. The comments above about the Old Testament (as well as those following about the New Testament) are largely from the perspective of Western (European) Christianity, largely driven by the Roman Catholic Church after its version of Christianity became the official religion of the Roman Empire and by churches derived from the Protestant Reformation. The portion of Christendom associated with the Orthodox churches[29] accepts the Apocrypha as Scripture (as does the Roman Catholic Church).

However, there are other parts of Christendom that have additions to both Old and New Testament not included in Protestant, Catholic, or Orthodox Scripture as well as not always including all books of the Protestant, Catholic, or Orthodox churches as Scripture.[30] Such is the situation with the Peshitta (accepted by many in the Syrian tradition which includes what some call the Nestorian Church[31]), the Armenian canon (Armenia was the first country to declare Christianity as its national religion, doing that half-a-century before Christianity became the official religion of the Roman Empire), the Coptic Bible, and the Scriptures used in Ethiopia.

No second century Christian writer shows knowledge of all 27 books in the New Testament by quotation or reference; and some also considered other books Scripture too. The first lists of just the 27 books of the New Testament and no others as Scripture do not appear until late in the fourth century (Athanasius and Councils of Laodicea, Hippo, and Carthage). This formal canonization of the New Testament occurs after Christianity had become acceptable as a religion within the Roman Empire (by the Edict of Milan in 313 A.D.) and then declared to be the official religion of the Roman Empire around 380 A.D. by Emperor Theodosius. This means that church leaders involved in the canonization process were acceptable to the Roman authorities; the impact of that political reality on the spiritual quality of the decisions by those leaders is unknown.

It is significant to note that the oldest relatively complete copies of the New Testament (*Codex Sinaiticus, Codex Vaticanus,* and *Codex Alexandrinus*) include or are thought to have included in missing sections Christian writings apparently considered Scripture in addition to the 27 books of the New Testament.[32] The purpose of this recitation of religious history is to make the point that in the early church (30s-240 A.D.) there were uncertainties about what writings were Christian Scripture (as noted earlier in the comments by Eusebius), but such uncertainties did not prevent God from working powerfully through the church. Those three codices also included much of the LXX with most of the Apocrypha as representation of Old Testament Scripture.

The bottom line about the canon of the New Testament: in the early church, especially the second century, there seems to have been significant differences about the books considered Scripture by different parts of Christendom.

3.2.1.3. Perspective about the Canon

It is helpful to remember that for a thousand years (from the time that the Vulgate became the official Bible of the Roman Catholic Church until the Protestant Reformation) that the Apocrypha was considered part of Christian Scripture in both Christendom's western manifestation (that of the Roman Catholic Church) and its eastern manifestation (in the various Orthodox churches and the Church of the East). It is good to consider what one reads or hears about the inspiration of Scripture and which books are Scripture in light of these historical realities. The historical realities noted earlier in this chapter suggest that in the early church there were uncertainties about which books are Scripture. Contemporary Christians should recognize uncertainties about which books should be considered Scripture instead of simply accepting what is only religious tradition since the Scripture itself does not specify which books are Scripture and no apostle or one directly taught by one or more of the apostles has listed as Scripture exactly the books currently considered to be Christian Scripture.

Since the late-fourth century, the 27 books of the New Testament have been accepted as Scripture by most of Western Christendom based upon church tradition (with only occasional complaints), a tradition begun by a collection of religious leaders acceptable to the politicized church and governmental leaders of the Roman Empire in the fourth century. Since that time, the Old Testament used by Catholic and Orthodox churches has included the Apocrypha. This too was based upon church tradition. The Protestant Reformation basically removed the Apocrypha from the Old Testament used by most Protestants (in part simply to make the distinction between Protestant and Catholic more evident).

Most Protestants are unaware that for more than two centuries after it was first translated all copies of the King James Version of the Bible included the Apocrypha (during that time the King James Version was the most widely used version of the Bible in English). The portion of Christendom generally called the Church of the East (including the Nestorian Church), which had many adherents during the first millennium of Christianity, had a looser perspective on Scripture and included things not accepted in Western churches and omitted things they included. During the first millennium of church history, the Church of the East may have had about a third of the Christian population in the world.[33]

Hence determination of which books should be included in the canon of Christian Scripture is not nearly so clear as some present it; and few of those who emphasize the importance of Scripture's inspiration consider church tradition as a very reliable guide to important spiritual truths.

CCR takes a very pragmatic approach to Scripture. What is important is God, the Father-Son-Holy Spirit Being, revealed by Scripture, and a person's relationship to Him. This is what allowed the early church, with its limited awareness of the New Testament and possible variations in the Old Testament, to be used so powerfully by God. It is the relationship to God that will allow Him to work powerfully through the church, not a particular belief about the book that reveals Him to people.

3.2.2. Content of Scriptural Materials

The previous section shows that there are uncertainties about which books should be considered Scripture (major sections of Christendom have different canons), and such uncertainties have existed since before the early church as well as within it. This section shows that there are similar uncertainties about the content of Scripture, as well as the uncertainties about which books are Scripture.

Many statements of belief about inspiration of Christian Scripture say that the original manuscripts (which often are called the "autographs") were what God inspired. Unfortunately, none of the autographs are available today; nor is information available today about the specific trail of copies from the autographs to any extant manuscript of Scripture. The original Old Testament manuscripts were written from about 1400 B.C. to 400 B.C. (to about 100 B.C. if all of the *Apocrypha* is included), and the original manuscripts of the 27 books of the New Testament were written 40-95 A.D.

The oldest copy of a relatively complete Hebrew Bible comes from about 900 A.D., with portions of the Hebrew Bible available in the Dead Sea Scrolls (most Dead Sea Scroll material is dated within a century or two before Christ). Scripture translations in several languages were made from a couple of centuries before Christ (the LXX) to several centuries after Christ (e.g., the Peshitta and early Latin and Coptic translations). Some copies of these translations come from as early as the fourth century A.D.

The earliest copies of a relatively complete Greek New Testament come from the fourth century, and there are manuscripts (including small ones) for about 40% of the Greek New Testament from before the end of the second century A.D. Hence for much of the Greek New Testament, multiple copies of passages exist that were made less than two-three centuries after the original. However, we have no information about the number of copies and their quality between the original manuscript and the oldest extant material available.

Because of the abundance of manuscripts available, the process of textual criticism[34] generally allows development of confidence that the basic context of New Testament passages can be established. This is an assumption; without explicit comparison with an original manuscript (i.e., an autograph), no evidential basis exists for the assumption although it is logically and emotionally appealing. It is clear that some passages (such as the end of Mark or the story of the woman caught in adultery) were not part of the original manuscripts of Scripture (i.e., the autographs).

This (belief or assumption about the relationship of extant materials to the autographs) is not based upon Scriptural statements. Scriptural statements talk about the original manuscripts being inspired by God; Scripture itself does not specifically address the copying process. Hence beliefs about reliability of copies of Scripture available today come from assumptions about how the Scriptural comments about the autographs can be extended to extant copies of the Scripture. Unfortunately, people may not think clearly and honestly about this subject. Application of what the Scripture says about the autographs is often misapplied to the copy of the Bible in a person's hand.

In this regard, CCR assumes (this perspective is not based upon a Scriptural comment since the Scripture itself does not address the relationship of the original inspired manuscripts to whatever copy one may have from that original) that textual criticism is able to produce a generally correct representation of what was in the original manuscripts. A "generally correct representation" is not the same as an absolutely accurate and correct representation; such a perfect representation does not exist (or if it should exist, we have no way to identify it from one that is imperfect).

Most modern translations of Christian Scripture are based upon the Hebrew and Aramaic text of the Old Testament and the Greek text of the New Testament that have been determined by application of textual criticism to extant manuscripts of the Scripture (and with consideration of implied textual readings from early translations of the Scripture such as the LXX and the early Latin and Syrian versions of the Bible).

Most versions of the Bible include an Introduction or Preface that presents the approach of the translation ("word-for-word," "thought-for-thought," or "paraphrase" are the three primary approaches), source of texts for the translation, and something about the history of the translation (such as its basis in an earlier translation and who the translators were).[35] Generally modern translations include a note when a significant change occurs from passages that long had been considered part of the Scripture (such as the end of Mark's Gospel, 16:9-20; the woman caught in adultery, John 7:53-8:11; part of 1 John 5:7; and the end of the model prayer, part of Matthew 6:13).

For the average Christian, simply trusting the Bible in his or her hands is the thing to do. CCR clear teachings provide a guide to boundaries on God's truth since CCR tenets seek to be derived from clear teaching found in multiple passages of undisputed portions of Scripture. CCR tenets can help one avoid ideas based upon obscure passages or ideas only supported by a single passage or ideas only supported by disputed portions of Scripture.

There is no knowledge of the path from the Scripture originals (i.e., the autographs) to the extant copies. How many copies were made and by whom, what kinds of copies later copies may have used, and how beliefs may have caused some copiers to modify the material they copied are not known. There are differences, some trivial and others significant, among extant copies of Scriptural materials (and among early translations of Scriptural material). While textual criticism provides reasonable assurance of what the text should be for most of the Scripture; some uncertainties exist.

For a trivial example of such textual uncertainty, consider the question of how tall Goliath was. As indicated in a previous endnote, the Masoretic Text of 1 Samuel 17:4 says Goliath was "six cubits and a span" tall (something over nine feet tall). A copy of this verse in Dead Sea Scroll Hebrew materials (which are a thousand years older than the oldest copy of the Masoretic Text) says Goliath was only "four cubits and a span" (about seven feet tall). The Septuagint also says Goliath was "four cubits and a span." The Septuagint (LXX) is the Greek translation of the Old Testament made a couple of centuries before Christ. The oldest complete copy of the LXX comes from the early fourth century. Septuagint fragments in the Dead Sea Scrolls from the Pentateuch and the Minor Prophets are dated a century or two before Christ. The first century Jewish historian, Josephus, also says Goliath was four cubits and a span tall. Which height for Goliath is Scripture (six cubits or four cubits plus a span)? There is no theological point of significance which depends upon the choice, other than possibly enhancing the reputation of David, the second king of the Jews in the Old Testament.

CCR assumes that the process of textual criticism provides a basic text of Scripture for which there are few significant uncertainties, even if some long accepted passages (such as the end of Mark's Gospel and the story of the woman caught in adultery found in John 8) are recognized as not being part of Scripture. Except for some unusual beliefs (such as the snake handling mentioned earlier), the text produced by textual criticism does not change the clear teachings of the Bible.

The bottom line about the text of Scriptural books: it is assumed that textual criticism can provide a generally reliable text of Scripture from the extant collection of manuscripts, but there will be some uncertainties about that generally reliable text of Scripture.

3.2.3. Proper Interpretation of Scripture

Martin Luther, the sparkplug of the Protestant Reformation, refused to accept hard and fast rules for interpretation of Scripture, especially rules that gave the church hierarchy final authority over the meaning of the Scripture (as indicated by his letters to Pope Leo X). This section does not contain such hard and fast rules, but it does provide perspectives that will help a person properly understand God's Word. There's an important aspect of proper interpretation of Scripture that is captured eloquently by a quote from Martin Luther: "No man understands the Scriptures, unless he be acquainted with the Cross" (a very true statement).[36] Church history is full of examples of significant things being done by people who felt God was speaking to them directly through the Scripture; some have called such an "inner light."[37]

Proper interpretation of Scripture recognizes both that Scripture is presented in normal human language (with the full variety of literal and figurative expressions) and that proper consideration must be given to the context in which the words of Scripture were spoken or written. This may introduce uncertainty in the meaning of a particular passage, but not in the basic teachings of the Scripture since such comes from multiple clear passages. The possibilities of misunderstanding (i.e., wrong beliefs) because figurative passages are taken literally are general well-known. For example, when a passage says that the number of people in a population is the same as the number of stars or as the grains of sand, it merely means that that there are a lot of people, not a specific number.[38]

The potential problem of failing to give passage context appropriate consideration is more difficult. Full knowledge of customs and ideals that affect the context may be lacking. Other times a contemporary context is assumed instead of one appropriate for when the passage was written. Failure to properly consider passage context can lead to inappropriate ideas. Sometimes the inappropriate idea will simply be a claim for support from a passage for an idea taught in Scripture but which that particular passage does not actually support.

This problem of misinterpretation is illustrated by a misinterpretation that this author long applied to Revelation 1:3. Revelations 1:3 promises a blessing to two kinds of people: those who read the prophecy of Revelation, and those who hear and obey that prophecy. This author erroneously took that verse as a promised blessing upon those who read that portion of God's Word, i.e., the book of Revelation (taking a contemporary perspective where most people are literate and copies of God's Word are plentiful and inexpensive). In its historical context, a very different meaning is clear. Although it is true that reading God's Word is a good thing to do and has many benefits, this verse does not promise a blessing for doing that. When this verse was written, few were literate (most scholars estimate literacy in the first century at 10-20% of the population). Also writing materials were expensive (because of Egypt's monopoly on papyrus, outside Egypt a sheet of papyrus roughly 16 inches square might cost a major portion of a common man's wages for a day[39]).

Consequently, most people were exposed to Scripture by it being read aloud in meetings. The blessing for the readers that John mentioned in Revelation 1:3 was not for reading Scripture privately, but for reading God's Word aloud in Christian services (the role of the person responsible for such reading was often mentioned in descriptions of Christian activities by early church writers). Paying attention to the historical context of Biblical passages can reduce some of the ideas that go beyond what the Scripture actually says. Failing to give appropriate attention to the historical context of a passage sometimes will merely lead to an inappropriate idea, i.e., an idea that the Bible does not really teach, and at other times might lead to beliefs that contradict clear teaching of Scripture.[40]

It is not uncommon for additional meanings to be attached to Scripture than which comes from its grammatical-historical interpretation (i.e., what is called its "literal meaning"), as described above. There are three basic kinds of the additional interpretation: allegorical, topological, and *sensus plenior*. Allegorical interpretation of Scripture looks beyond its literal meaning to seek a spiritual meaning, and was extensively used from the early church to the present.[41] Topological interpretation, is sometimes considered a subset of allegorical interpretation; topological interpretation looks for types of Christ and His activities in the people and events of the Old Testament. Its focus is teaching moral lessons or illustrations that provide insights about Christ. Some of the insights suggested by allegorical and topological interpretation have been very helpful to people without leading them astray from truths revealed by literal interpretation of the Scripture, but sometimes suggestions from such an interpretation go beyond (or even contradict) what is clearly taught in Scripture. Hence allegorical or topological interpretations should be approached very cautiously and always constrained by clear teachings from the literal interpretation of Scripture.

"*Sensus plenior*" (Latin for "fuller sense" or "fuller meaning") is used in Biblical interpretation to describe the supposed deeper meaning intended by God but perhaps not intended by the human author. It is thought that Andre Fernandez coined the term in 1927, which was popularized by Roman Catholic theologian Raymond E. Brown in the 1950s publication of his doctoral dissertation on the subject. He defines *sensus plenior* as "That additional, deeper meaning, intended by God but not clearly intended by the human author, which is seen to exist in the words of a biblical text (or group of texts, or even a whole book) when they are studied in the light of further revelation or development in the understanding of revelation."[42]

There are a number of instances of *sensus plenior* in Scripture when the Scripture itself identifies a fuller significance in an earlier passage of Scripture as explained by a later passage of Scripture. For example, Jesus did this in the Sermon on the Mount as He extended the meaning of the commandment against murder to include prohibition against hate and disrespect, and the commandment against adultery to include a prohibition on lust (Matthew 5). Because of the Holy Spirit's guidance for those whom God chose to produce the Scripture, such interpretation of the fuller sense of those passages is correct and can be accepted as true since all Scripture is accepted as truth from God. And that is where the problem arises with *sensus plenior*. How can anyone other than one God has chosen to produce the Scripture be sure an interpretation of the fuller sense of a Scripture passage is correct, and not just the fancy of the interpreter?[43]

Potential for abuse of the *sensus plenior* concept is obvious, but so is the reality of it in Scripture. It has to be considered in proper Scriptural interpretation. Addressing the hermeneutical challenge of *sensus plenior* fully is beyond the scope of this book, although there is a greater discussion of it in Appendix C; here it simply is noted that such is a critical aspect of proper Scriptural interpretation.[44]

Several Protestant oriented discussions of *sensus plenior* have been referenced in the endnotes. Since the term *sensus plenior* and development of it initially in the 20th century started in Catholic circles, it is appropriate to see a contemporary expression of it within Catholicism. Such is available from Pauline A. Viviano, "The Senses of Scripture," *National Bible Week 2015* (available at http://www.usccb.org/bible/national-bible-week/upload/viviano-senses-scripture.pdf accessed September 2017).[45]

3.2.3.1. Pernicious Interpretation

Alexander Pope's 1711 poem (*An Essay on Criticism*) contains a line in its 744 lines that has been used by notable politicians such as Edmund Burke and Abraham Lincoln as well as by numerous musicians and others. Of course, that line says "fools rush in where angels fear to tread." Some may apply such to comments here.

The previous section talked about proper interpretation of Scripture and made suggestions about appropriate ways to approach the Scripture; that section was based upon the unstated assumption that one approached the Scripture as normal communication. Unfortunately some approach the Scripture in a different way. They come at it (and at religion and spiritual matters in general) through a lens of an overarching ideology. This book calls that approach "pernicious interpretation."

One lexicon defined "pernicious" as "1) causing insidious harm or ruin, ruinous, injurious, hurtful; 2) deadly, fatal; and 3) Obsolete: evil, wicked." Such is pernicious interpretation.

For about a thousand years before the Reformation that sprang from Martin Luther's conflicts with the Roman Catholic Church, allegorical methods often were used in Scriptural interpretation. Such were used in association with more literal and standard approaches to interpretation for most of the Scripture. Some of the ideas produced by allegorical interpretation were quite fanciful and have long since been discarded, but other ideas persist in the ideology of some groups.[46] Allegorical interpretation is not necessarily pernicious; but allegorical interpretation poses the same kind of interpretative problem as topological interpretation and *sensus plenior*.

What this book calls "pernicious interpretation" arose much later; it came out of the enlightenment and modernity. A pernicious interpretation of Scripture has one dominant trait: it approaches the Scripture from an over-riding philosophical perspective that causes everything to be twisted by the lens of that perspective. There are many such philosophical perspectives. Some are very obvious: that of Liberation Theology and feminist ideology have been given a great deal of publicity. Others may focus on a theory of literary development, political and social ideals, or even cultural identity. Whether applied in large to the whole Scripture, or just to a more restricted portion of it (such as efforts to make all Scriptural references to God gender-neutral as some have done), such interpretations are pernicious.

Pernicious interpretation of Scripture has a second significant characteristic, and it may even be more important than the dominant trait just noted. That characteristic is that people are the measure of all things in pernicious interpretation; i.e., this is the essence of secularism. It also is a basis of modern idolatry (the worship of the creature instead of the Creator). The over-arching philosophies (or perspectives) that dominate in pernicious interpretation derive from ideas of the importance of human equality and tolerance, of the supreme authority of human achievements and scientific accomplishments, of utopian social and political ideals, etc. A wide variety of labels have been attached to the various approaches; some of which are positive or neutral (such as liberal or modern) and others of which are pejorative. This book does not address pernicious interpretation in more detail; it merely warns that pernicious interpretation is dangerous. This is in keeping with the warnings in the New Testament about false teachings; that false teaching is a very pervasive problem is indicated by the abundance of warnings against such in the New Testament (e.g., Matthew 7:15 & 24:11; Acts 20:29-30; Romans

16:17-18; 2 Corinthians 11:13-15; Galatians 1:8; Colossians 2:8; 2 Timothy 4:3-4; Titus 1:6-16; 1 John 4:1-6; 2 Peter 3:14-18).

3.2.3.2. Interpretation Limitations

It is important to understand that proper interpretation has limitations. First, God has not chosen to reveal everything that a person might want to know in Scripture. There are many details related to the Messiah's first coming that were not revealed in the Old Testament, just as there are many details related to the Messiah's second coming that have not been revealed in either the Old or New Testament. Not even the most elaborate explanations of Scriptural prophecy, or even the collection of all explanations of Scriptural prophecy, reveal every detail of Christ's return. It is a situation similar to what the Apostle John said at the end of his Gospel about the things Jesus did in His first coming as the Messiah: John wrote "Now there are also many other things that Jesus did [things John did not mention in his Gospel]. Were every one of them to be written, I suppose that the world itself could not contain the books that would be written." (John 21:25 ESV)

Second, some make exaggerated claims for Scripture. Some have claimed that the Scripture provides specific guidance for every situation a person might face. The Scripture never claims that and the claim is not true. The Scripture provides both general and detailed guidance for those seeking to please God in the way they live; but that guidance does not always provide the detailed guidance that one needs in deciding what to do. The person must be attuned to the working of God's Spirit in the person's mind so that correct decisions can be made (ala Romans 12:1-2),

This issue is more complicated than some assume because there are things the Scripture does not address in detail. For example, the Scripture does not say how to decide what tires to buy when the tires on a person's vehicle need to be replace: should the best quality ones, which are more expensive, be bought, or should lower quality ones which are less expensive be bought? In addition, some situations demand action based upon conflicting guidance from the Scripture. For example, the Scripture says God expects His people to be generous in providing help for the needy and the Scripture also says God expects His people to act with prudence in regard to material possessions.

Third, some things are beyond sure understanding. The classic example of this is Matthew 2:23 about the return of the child Jesus and His parents from Egypt: "and he [Joseph] went and lived in a town called Nazareth. So was fulfilled what was said through the prophets, that He [Jesus, the Messiah] would be called a Nazarene." (ESV) The meaning of this verse looks straightforward. The problem is that no single passage in the Old Testament says the Messiah would be a Nazarite or from Narareth (two possible explanations of what the verse was intended to mean). Two other possible explanations are put forth. One possibility says that those from Nazareth were generally despised by most Jews of the time for various reasons (as illustrated by Philip's comment in John 1:46, "Can anything good come out of Nazareth?") and thus fulfilled multiple Old Testament prophecies that the Messiah would be despised. The other possibility says that Nazarene (vocally) is similar to the Hebrew word for "branch" and there are several Old Testament prophecies about the Messiah as God's branch.

The Scripture is God's truth, and so what Matthew 2:23 says is true. However, it is unclear exactly what it means. Many things in the Scripture are very clear, especially truths that are presented repeatedly in multiple parts of the Scripture; but there are also things in the Scripture (such as Matthew 2:23) whose meaning is not so clear. Wise people focus on the clear teachings, and never make interpretation of unclear things a basis for division among the followers of Jesus.

An aside for the reader who is curious about why no reference is made to how the early church addressed Matthew 2:23 since this book has placed so much emphasis upon emulating the early church as a way to promote the spiritual unity Jesus prayed for. The reason the book makes no reference to how the early church addressed Matthew 2:23 is that there does not seem to be any comments about that verse by early church writers.[47]

Thus, in summary, there are three basic limitations on Scriptural interpretation: 1) the Scripture does not address everything, 2) the meaning of some passages of Scripture is unclear, and 3) the meaning of Scripture can be distorted by false teaching. Recognition of these limitations will help one to deal with the Scripture appropriately.

3.3. Interactions of Spiritual Aspects and Material Aspects of Reality

Some wrongly posit that spiritual aspects of reality are distinct from its material aspects. First, spiritual aspects of reality interact with material aspects of reality at times; miracles in Christian Scripture are examples of such interactions. Material aspects of reality (i.e., stuff with atoms and subatomic particles) may be involved in spiritual aspects such as heaven and beings like angels or demons; whether or not that is the case is not known.

The Scripture describes people in several different ways. Sometimes the person is treated as a unitary whole (even when just part of the person is mentioned). Sometimes the person is described as having two parts: body and soul, or body and spirit (sometimes this contrasts the material and the spiritual). And sometimes the person is described as having three parts: spirit (which connects the person to God – dead until the new birth), soul (basically what is called the personality: intellect, emotion, and volition, which many designate as "will"), and body. Interaction between the body and soul has long been known (some illnesses are designated psychosomatic); modern technology is enabling modern medicine to have much better understanding of some of the interactions between body and soul. Physical and mental behaviors are believed to be generally controlled by what happens in a person's brain. However caution is needed since the brain has 80 billion neutrons, each with thousands of possible connections and the brain sometimes changes the way it processes things (when injured or otherwise impacted). Hence what is known to be a relation between something and a response in a particular situation may not be that for everyone at all times. Some of what is written about neuroscience and related subjects fails to recognize or acknowledge such and erroneously presents a more deterministic perspective than is realistic. Science is often as negligent in dealing with its uncertainties as some claim religion is; unfortunately, "pot calling the kettle black" behavior is very common and occurs among those in most camps.

Interaction between the spirit and the material aspects of a person (i.e., body and soul) is nebulous. Such interactions are not clearly understood and may not appear to occur consistently because people cannot perceive all pertinent factors of the interaction (the Scripture is not a textbook that fully explains such – it says some things, but leaves much unaddressed). Little is known about spiritual creatures (such as angels and demons) and about how such and other spiritual influences can interact with the material world (including people) to allow us to make anything other than anecdotal comments about such things as miraculous healings (like Jesus did with the man born blind), demonic possession and exorcism, or other interactions between the spiritual and material realms. Obviously there are many false and exaggerated claims from all sides (e.g., those who blame every bad thing on demons and those who deny the possibility of any kind of miraculous intervention, i.e., one stimulated by non-material factors).

Human limitations in perception of spiritual interactions is illustrated by the fact, as noted previously, that theologians have not been able to determine how to determine who the Elect are on earth with complete accuracy in spite of working on that issue for centuries. It will be easy to identify the Elect in heaven (they will be the ones who are there); their identification on earth, however, is not so certain.

The Scripture only has a few hints about spiritual aspects of reality apart from that which involves people. The Scripture does not explain God's relationship with other creatures; some take that silence to mean God does not have a personal (spiritual) relationship with creatures other than humans. However, Scripture hints at the existence of such relationships (e.g., trees singing praise to God in 1 Chronicles 16).[48] Likewise the Scripture hints that there are varieties of spiritual beings that we know little or nothing about (e.g., cherubim and seraphim). It is very dangerous to draw conclusions from the absence of information.

Some mistakenly assume that God's interaction in human affairs is driven only by what people do. Certainly the Scripture indicates that God acts in response to what people do, and it is clear that He has the right to do whatever He wishes with His creation. The Apostle Paul makes this clear in Romans 9, where he uses the example of the potter's right to do what he wishes with the clay to illustrate the right of God to do as He wishes with His creation. That point comes after Paul says God did something many people consider atrocious. He chose to love one person and hate another before they were born, before they had done anything good or bad.

This kind of idea troubles many people. It requires limitations of human perception to be faced. People seldom fully know all pertinent circumstances. God does. Human judgment is faulty at times. God's judgment is never faulty. He always makes the right decision. Job provides a great example; Job glorified God for His greatness and His righteousness, even when God seemed to be doing to be doing something wrong. God never does anything wrong. Full understanding of a situation will reveal the propriety of God's actions.

Such ideas appear in both Old and New Testaments. Isaiah 64:8 calls people the clay and God the potter. Jeremiah 18 uses the analogy of the potter in Jeremiah's eleventh prophecy. The Apostle Paul says similar things in Romans 9. These passages indicate God's power over the world and all in it as well as His right to act as He chooses.

The book of Job brings a new dimension to the interaction of the spiritual and material aspects of reality. The first two chapters of Job indicate that spiritual interactions in our material reality may be stimulated by things outside the material world. In the book of Job, those things are the inter-actions between God and Satan, which led to raids by the Sabeans and the Chaldeans along with fire from heaven to destroy Job's possessions and a great wind that collapsed a house killing Job's children. When people look to the behavior of people and nations to explain their calamities and successes, they may not be able to find the correct answer because the causes for such may not be based in such behavior. This aspect of spir-itual interaction with the material aspects of reality is often overlooked.

This aspect of history is seldom addressed in any history. That includes histories of individuals (such as biographies), religious histories (such as church histories), and general secular histories that deal with nations, special topics such as technology history or various social histories that address particular topics such as suffrage or unionization. It is easy to understand why such is not even mentioned since people have no way of knowing anything about such unless God chooses to reveal it as He did in the book of Job. Because CCR assumes God can do things in the universe now as He chooses to do so, that requires consideration of such, and recognition that such can happen.

A few comments about the possibility of miracles are pertinent. Miracles (when defined as something which cannot be explained by materialistic processes, and perhaps even appears to contradict usual materialistic processes) can be thought of as insertion of energy into a situation. For example, in the situation where Jesus gave an adult man who had been born blind his sight, that miracle could have occurred from insertion of energy that modified the molecular structures and neutron connections within the man's brain.

Christian Scripture indicates that the spiritual aspect of reality can pro-vide such energy (creation itself shows that); every miracle described in the Scripture (from those restricted to a single person such as bringing a dead body to life or healing an individual's illness to those involving great material impact such as dividing the Red Sea for the Jewish exodus from Egypt or destruction of Jericho's walls) could be explained by insertion of additional energy into the situation. There is no scientific proof that such energy insertions from the spiritual aspects of reality are impossible. No scientific measurements were made at creation (the Big Bang in contemporary scientific terminology). No scientific measurements of totally energy at a miracle have been made to show such additional insertion of energy could not have happened. Hence contention and claims that miracles are impossible are not scientific findings; such are merely assertions of assumption based upon materialistic prejudice.

3.4. Conundrums from Reality's Infinite Aspects

CCR accepts the infinite nature of God. Information about things that are infinite does not always comply with the limits of finite reasoning. This is illustrated by mathematics. The Cantor Point Set in Infinite Set Theory allows a line segment to be thrown away while being kept.[49] Such is totally impossible in finite mathematics, but acceptable in infinite mathematics. In infinite mathematics, something can be Not-A and A at the same time; a complete impossibility in finite mathematics as we all know.

At times contradictory things (similar to the things noted above for infinite mathematics) are said about God in the Scripture. Such things cannot be pigeon-holed within the constraints of finite reasoning. All that can be done is to clearly state the simultaneous contradictory aspects of God's reality. This is illustrated by fundamental truths about the Godhead such as its Triune Godhead (Father-Son-Holy Spirit, Three Persons One God), the Divine-Human Nature of the Son of God, the simultaneous choosing by God before creation of those who would be saved and the necessity of the individual choice to believe in Jesus for salvation (i.e., free will), etc.

Contradictory things the Scripture says about God and His creation also are some of the ideas that thoughtful people have great trouble with. The fact that the Scripture says God is both all-powerful and good while recognizing the evil present in the world (such as the 2017 massacre in Las Vegas by a deranged individual shooting into a crowd from a hotel window or the calamities from natural events such as earthquakes, hurricanes, and floods) is one of the major stumbling blocks for many spiritually. CCR sees such as conundrums from the infinite character of reality; and does not try to justify such because such justification is beyond the capability of human finite conceptions and expressions.

At times God's actions come across as contradictory because of limited human perception of all factors involved in the situation. At times, God says He will do something or that something will happen; then God "repents" and changes what He said would happen.[50] CCR accepts by faith that such actions are consistent with God's nature even if they appear contradictory because of limited human perception of everything involved. CCR understands that the infinite reality of God and His actions cannot be forced into the pigeon-holes of finite reasoning.

An analogy that may be helpful is what might have happened when an African native in the 19th century who had no knowledge of modern medicine brought his sick child to a medical missionary. The medical missionary diagnoses the child as suffering from acute appendicitis. He needs to operate to save the child's life. To the African native, it appears the missionary is doing bad things. First, he seems to kill the child (administers anesthesia). Then he starts to mutilate the child's body, cutting it open and taking part of it out. In fact, the medical missionary is saving the sick child's life. It just looks wrong to the African native because of his lack of knowledge. Often God's actions may seem as wrong to us as the medical missionary's actions might have seemed to the African native. We need to trust that God always does things right.

Such conundrums trouble many serious and thoughtful believers; CCR appreciates the danger that potential abuse of conceptions and ideas in the process poses as well as the potential for ideas that people find unsettling. Keeping clear revelation about the righteous nature of God firmly in mind helps to minimize potential conceptual abuse.

Speculation about God's purpose in creating humanity with choice ("free will" in theological terminology) can lead to sobering, even disturbing concepts when such speculations do not try to pigeonhole God into the constraints of finite reasoning. For example, some have thought that possibly God created fallible people so that His plan of redemption could allow God, a holy Being Who is the source of all life, to experience things that seem incompatible with His nature in a way that did not compromise Him. The Scripture says God's plan of redemption caused the Son, the Second Person of the Triune Godhead, to become sin and experience death (see Paul's epistle to the Romans for discussion of God's plan of redemption); and somehow this was done without compromising the holiness or life of God. From some perspectives, this speculation magnifies God's love since it makes it seem that God was willing to put His very character and perhaps even His existence at risk in order to make salvation possible for people. Even some seminary graduates have described this as a new thought for them.

CCR believes this approach (accepting conundrums that arise from God's infinite aspects) is essential for proper dealing with God's truth and believes that some of the differences espoused within Christendom arise from failure to accept some of the conceptual contradictions stemming from God's infinite nature. One group would emphasize one aspect of such contradictions and another group would emphasize a different aspect; and a split would result.

Chapter 4.

SELECTED CCR TENETS

THE FIFTH CCR principle is that basic beliefs of Classic Christian Realism (CCR) come from clear teachings of the Scripture in multiple passages. That principle includes a restriction on the source of clear teachings to "undisputed books of Scripture." Before selected tenets of CCR are presented, it is appropriate to explain what is meant by undisputed books of Scripture and to identify specifically the disputed and undisputed books so that it will be clear where CCR draws its tenets from. The previous chapter discussed uncertainties about which books are in the canon, but did not explicitly present the CCR position on such. The previous chapter also discussed uncertainties about the text of Scripture and its interpretation.

4.1. What Is Meant by Undisputed Books in Scripture?

Nearly everything thing religious, including Christian Scripture, has been called into question by someone at some time for some reason. Often such reasons are of questionable validity; but that does not prevent the question being raised. Hence, to take "undisputed" in its most literal and extreme sense, there are no undisputed books of Christian Scripture. Questions have been raised about every bit of possible Christian Scripture. However, "undisputed" is used in more ways than just its most literal and extreme sense. "Undisputed" is much more frequently taken to mean "generally agreed upon," "accepted," or something similar.

There are differences in the books considered Scripture by different groups within Christendom. The lists of books considered Scripture by Protestant groups, the Roman Catholic Church, and various Orthodox churches are not identical. Others, such as the church in Ethiopia, have yet a different list of Scriptural books. This is not a new problem. It existed in the early church, and continued to be so after the early church if one takes a world view of Christendom and not just the Western perspective of the Roman Catholic Church. This is illustrated by content of the Peshitta (the Scripture of the Church of the East), which does not include four of the general epistles or Revelation but has most of the Apocrypha. Exact dates of origin for the Peshitta are uncertain; its Old Testament portions probably originated about the first century and the New Testament material in the second century. This variety of Scriptural books made use of terms like "accepted" or "recognized" inappropriate since such could not be applied universally to all segments of Christendom (even if one excluded the groups some call Christian that originated in modern times, such as the Mormons, from consideration along with the writings that they consider Scripture which are not viewed that way by other groups). Hence CCR uses the adjective "undisputed" as the description of Scripture from which CCR clear teachings will be taken. In doing this, "undisputed" is taken to mean "generally accepted" or "generally agreed upon." The books considered "undisputed" Scripture here (as specified in the following section) are basically accepted in all major segments of modern Christendom AND none of them were considered heretical by the early church, although there were questions about some (as noted in the following section). Some were both accepted and questioned at the same time (for example, the fourth century church historian Eusebius has Revelation in both the accepted and spurious categories in discussion of the canon of Scripture).

4.2. Undisputed Books in Scripture

For CCR, writings that are accepted as Scripture without significant dispute must be specified since those are the writings from which clear teachings of Scripture must come. This does not mean that CCR considers disputed books in Scripture not to be Scripture or encourages others to view such that way (determination of their status as Scripture is outside the scope of this book); people may find items listed as disputed Scripture to be helpful, and even treat such as guidance from God, but CCR will not use material from disputed Scripture in developing CCR's clear teachings of Scripture. Some may consider this approach to the Scriptural status of disputed books to be pusillanimous, but to address that topic in reasonable detail so that it is treated fairly would distract from the primary purpose of this book.

4.2.1. Undisputed Books of the Old Testament

The *Apocrypha* is accepted as Scripture by major segments of Christendom (Roman Catholics, Orthodox churches, Peshitta, et al) and may have been considered Scripture by Jews in the Diaspora in the first century because such was part of the LXX. However it is not clear that those books were accepted as Scripture by first century Jews in Judea, even though books from the *Apocrypha* are among materials in the Dead Sea Scrolls and it appears that Jews in the Roman Province of Syria (which includes Galilee, Samaria, and Judea) and in Egypt used the LXX as well as Hebrew Scripture (and the LXX includes the Apocrypha). Hence CCR does not include the *Apocrypha* in its undisputed books of Scripture.

This exclusion of the *Apocrypha* is not expected to impact any major belief of historic Christianity even though it removes Jewish history from about 400 B.C. to the time of Christ from Scriptural records. That history denotes God's assistance in battle during the time of the Maccabees (second century B.C.) in ways similar to that reported in the historical books of the Protestant Old Testament.

Some express concern about the Scriptural character of the eight books of the 39 in the Protestant Old Testament that are not explicitly quoted or referenced by New Testament writers; these books are Ruth, Ezra, Esther, Ecclesiastes, Song of Solomon, Lamentations, Obadiah, and Zephaniah. However, these eight books are included in the Masoretic Text of the Hebrew Bible, in the LXX, and in early Latin, Syrian, and Coptic translations of the Bible. This author is not aware that any in the early church questioned their Scriptural character. Hence all the books of the Masoretic Text (which basically are the books in the Protestant Old Testament) are accepted as undisputed books of Scripture.

It should be noted that no part of Esther is contained in the Dead Sea Scrolls. Esther is the only book in the Protestant Old Testament and the Hebrew Bible based upon the Masoretic Text from which there are no manuscript portions in the Dead Sea Scrolls.

CCR does not consider books beyond those of the Protestant Old Testament and the Apocrypha to be undisputed Scripture of the Old Testament even if such are accepted as canonical by some portion of Christendom (such as the Ethiopian Orthodox Church).

4.2.2. Undisputed Books of the New Testament

Scriptural character of seven books of the traditional 27 in the New Testament was questioned by some in the early church. These included Hebrews and Revelation, which CCR accepts as part of the undisputed Scripture for clear teaching. Reasons for accepting Hebrews and Revelation are shown below.

Hebrews was questioned mainly because its author was not specified and could not be determined; that is not considered to be an adequate reason to exclude Hebrews from Scripture used for clear teachings in CCR. The first reference to Hebrews is by Clement of Rome about 96 A.D. and a copy of it is in the oldest major papyrus of New Testament material P46 (dated late-second century)[51]. Hebrews seems to have been generally accepted as Scripture by the early church. While many have attributed Hebrews to Paul, it seems unlikely that he was its authority. In the third century, the noted Christian scholar Origen (184-254 A.D.) had this to say about the authorship of Hebrews: "Whoever wrote the epistle, God only knows for sure." Tertullian (150-220 A.D.) suggested Barnabas (the only person other than Paul suggested by name during the early church from extant materials). Later there are numerous suggestions: Apollos, Luke, Clement of Alexandria, Priscilla (she was only suggested as a possibility for authorship of Hebrews in modern times; her long association with Paul could have caused her to write so similarly to Paul that such caused many to think Paul actually was the author of Hebrews), and several others.

As noted previously, Eusebius listed Revelation as both accepted and spurious. The author of Revelation identifies himself as "John" four times in Revelation (1:1, 4, 9; 2:8). That the author was John the Apostle is noted by several second century writers (Justin Martyr, Melito, and Irenaeus) and by prominent Christians of the third century (Tertullian, Hippolytus, Clement of Alexandria, and Origen). All treated the book as Scripture. Dionysius of Alexandria considered Revelation Scripture but about 255 A.D. commented that some (whom he did identify) had doubts about Revelation and that he thought it was not the Apostle John but some other John who wrote Revelation. Arguments against Revelation as Scripture in the early church concerned its authorship and the sense that it emphasized an earthly kingdom instead of the heavenly one. The weight of the evidence from the early church strongly supports Revelation as Scripture; so CCR accepts it as a source for clear teachings from the Scripture.

The other five books that were questioned by some in the early church (James, 2nd & 3rd epistles of John, 2nd Peter, and Jude) are excluded from Scripture used for clear teachings by CCR mainly because of such attitudes about them in the early church.

None of the books that some in the early church may have considered Scripture but which were not included in what has been the traditional canon of the New Testament by Western Christianity (e.g., the non-canonical items in the three codices mentioned in the previous chapter) are considered undisputed Scriptural sources for CCR clear teachings. It is worth noting that none of those items that were considered by some as Scripture (or which may be included in the Scripture of Orthodox churches, the other Eastern expressions of Christianity, the Ethiopian canon, etc.) are considered Scripture by every one of those groups.

4.2.3. Comments about Clear Teachings from Undisputed Scripture

For completeness, none of the books first suggested as Scripture by some after the early church are considered Scripture. This includes a wide variety of materials from both modern and ancient time. Such include not only things like books suggested by the Mormons as Scripture but also church traditions that are given equal status with Scripture as sources for belief and practice.

The CCR specification of undisputed Scripture eliminates about 10% of the books in the Protestant Bible and all of the books contained in Catholic and Orthodox Bibles (and other groups reaching back to antiquity such as the Church of the East and the Ethiopian church) which are not in the Protestant Bible; however restriction of CCR beliefs to clear teachings from these "undisputed" portions of Scripture are not expected to move CCR beliefs outside the realm of historic Christian beliefs. CCR makes no claim that the books it does not accept as undisputed Scripture are unreliable; only that CCR will not use them for its "clear teachings" from Scripture.

4.3. Selected CCR Tenets

Basic CCR tenets deal mainly with spiritual aspects of reality, and are derived from clear teachings of Christian Scripture. As noted before, clear teachings of Scripture are drawn from undisputed portions of Scripture.

The previous section identified which books of Scripture are considered undisputed by CCR. The texts of those books used for establishment of clear teachings by CCR have been affirmed by textual criticism as a reasonable approximation of the autographs they represent. The clear teachings identified by CCR have support in multiple passages of undisputed Scripture and are derived by sound principles of Scriptural interpretation.

The six CCR tenets presented in this book address 1) God, 2) His plan of salvation, 3) the Scripture, 4) people, 5) the church, and 6) a God-pleasing life. Since this book is only an initial exposure to CCR and it is presented primarily from the author's personal perspective, fuller development of CCR and its tenets in a more formal way is expected to be done by other publications, which probably will also address other topics.

CCR faces the same challenge that every summary of Christian belief faces. That challenge is how to state the belief clearly and with reasonable logical/philosophical completeness and coherence that does not go beyond what the Scripture actually says. This is a special challenge when dealing with theological topics because God is infinite; limitations on expressing infinite things appropriately in finite language constrained by finite reasoning makes this very difficult.

As note previously, mathematics illustrates this difficulty. Things impossible in finite mathematics are possible in infinite mathematics. The same kinds of conundrums apply in dealing with the infinite truth about God. Truths about the infinite God may seem contradictory and impossible to human finite reasoning capabilities. This shows in well-known elements of Christian theology. God is Three in One. The Son of God is both divine and human. God has chosen those who will be saved before the foundation of the earth and each person that will be saved has to believe in Jesus Christ. Often Christians have split because one group emphasized one aspect of an infinite truth and another group emphasized a different aspect of an infinite truth.

The Scripture explicitly warns not to add to or take away from it (Deuteronomy 4:2 & 12:32; Revelation 22:18). The Apostle Paul even makes a vague warning about not going beyond what is written (1 Corinthians 4:6). Such can be hard to do when trying to describe a Scriptural doctrine in a comprehensive way. Unfortunately church history has many instances of divisions among followers of Jesus when all involved would affirm the specific things the Scripture said but then all could not agree on the wording of their synopsis and summary of that doctrine; sometimes in that kind of situation one group would condemn and anathematize the others. This is especially a problem when the infinite attributes of God cause aspects of God's truth to appear contradictory, and some emphasize one aspect over others instead of simply accepting all aspects presented in Scripture as true.

The approach CCR takes to the theological conundrums that arise from God's infinite nature is to affirm all aspects of revealed truth, even when those aspects appear to be irreconcilable. Three and One are different; yet Scripture reveals God is both. How can a person "choose" to believe that Jesus in the Savior if God has already chosen (or not chosen) that person to be part of the Elect? CCR simply affirms both the selection by God of those who would be saved before creation and the responsibility of the individual to believe in Jesus for salvation. CCR accepts that such a position has aspects that defy human logic; but CCR believes this is the only way to be fully compliant with truth revealed in Scripture.

CCR seeks to deal with God's truth as presented by Christian Scripture as honestly and appropriately as possible. Of the six topics addressed below, two are primary (God and His plan of salvation), the other four, although each is very important, are secondary. Keeping that priority clear was what allowed the early church to maintain its spiritual unity in spite of adverse circumstances and that unity seems to have facilitated God's powerful working through the early church. Keeping priorities proper is also the key for individuals and organizations in using their lives and resources in ways that please God most and which conform most closely to His will for them.

CCR accepts only Christian Scripture as reliable revelation of God's truth with general applicability to all people. Hence, CCR does not give the same authority to guidance from other sources, such as church tradition or prophetic utterances. Sometimes guidance from such sources can be helpful, particularly in regard to specific circumstances, and other times such guidance may be contrary to God's will (especially when such "guidance" is contrary to clear Scriptural teachings, as when people are tortured and killed for heresy instead of simply avoiding them). Since Scripture itself does not specifically identify what writings are Scripture or say that such revelation from God stops after a particular time; such is simply based on assumption (it is not something specifically stated by Scripture).

4.3.1. God

CCR tenets begin with God Who has revealed Himself and His activities through His creation, through direct communication with people (by dreams, visions, visitations which some call theophanies, through the working of God's Spirit in a person's mind to affect the person's thinking), through His Son when He lived on earth, and through the Christian Scripture (written guidance of general applicability to all peoples at all times – the Scripture also contains all the extant reliable information about what Jesus said and did while He lived on the earth).

Such "direct communications" with people by God reported in the Scripture do not occur uniformly in the 1,500 years from Moses to death of the last of the Twelve Apostles or nor geography; instead such "direct communications" happen at God's choosing. Some contend that such "direct communications" (as well as miracles, speaking in tongues, and other unusual things) ceased with passing of the apostles; but the Scripture does not claim such ceased at that time. There are numerous accounts of such "direct communications" continuing throughout church history in many varieties of Christianity and throughout the entire world. Of course, some of the reports are unreliable; but some have all the earmarks of truthful reports (some have even been approached very scientifically, such as procedures employed by the Catholic Church to verify miracles associated with those being considered for classification as a saint). This author thinks it is very unlikely that all claims of direct communication from God since the apostles died are phony. *Protestants,* Alec Ryrie's book of 500 years of Protestant history (a book called "the best recent history" of Protestants in a monumental 6-page article about Protestants in the November 4-10, 2017 issue of the noted news periodical *The Economist*), mentions claims of such direct communication from God by people from teenagers to old folks in many different kinds of churches throughout most of the time since Martin Luther and from around the world; many church histories largely ignore or simply dismiss such claims and examples of "direct communication" from God.

God has created all that is (spiritual and material) and sustains it; He is infinite, eternal, omnipotent (nothing is impossible for Him), omniscient, and omnipresent as well as good, righteous, holy, just, merciful, gracious, and loving.

God does many impossible things. He created the universe from nothing. Jesus used the impossibility of a camel going through the eye of a needle as an example of an impossible thing that God can do (by saving sinful man). From this author's perspective, the most impossible thing that God has done that Scripture reveals is the way He saves sinful people. That required the holy God to become sin for us and the source of life to die; truly nothing is impossible for the God Who can do such. May God expand our understanding of what it means for nothing to be impossible for God. Perhaps God created the universe as He did (so that the universe created by a good and all-powerful Creator had evil in it, a situation that disturbs many thoughtful people) so that He could experience something otherwise impossible for Him (a holy God the source of all life being contaminated with evil as He became sin for us and experiencing death as He made human salvation possible and doing so without compromising His essential holiness). Nothing is impossible for God.

From some perspectives, God is not just. He forgives the sins of individuals, letting another (Jesus) pay their penalty. In one sense justice is satisfied; but in another sense, any expression of mercy is unjust. A wise person accepts how God acts as just to help that person properly understand the concept of being just instead of criticizing God for failing to comply with the person's perspective on just behavior.

This is hard for many to do. They may not realize how foolish and wrong it is to elevate one's reasoning and standards to a position above God, which is what they do in judging God's behavior. It is a subtle form of idolatry, making the creature and the creature's perceptions superior to God. God, the creator of all that is, is not subject to whims of His creation. He does not have to explain His actions; and the book of Job makes that clear. At the end of the book, God and Job communicate. Job wants to know why his woes have come. God does not explain to Job why things had happened; instead God reveals His greatness to Job and Job's insignificance as a creature God had made. Job, righteous man that he was, got the point. He was disgusted with himself for being so foolish as to seek an accounting from God, as revealed by Job 42:1-6.

The One God is the Three Person Being (Father, Son, and Holy Spirit) which many call Trinity. God continues to be involved in His creation; He may use processes people understand (such as the laws of biology, chemistry, and physics) or processes people do not understand (which are often called "miracles"). God is not limited by the finite conceptions and reasoning of humans.

Jesus says explicitly that God is Spirit, and those who worship must worship Him in spirit and truth (John 4:24), but neither in that discussion or elsewhere in Scripture is the relationship between the spiritual aspects of reality and the material aspects of reality explained. It is clear that spiritual aspects of reality can impact the material, as demonstrated by creation and by miracles; however what role material aspects of reality may have in the spiritual realm is not revealed. It is unknown if atoms and subatomic particles are in the bodies of angels or demons, or in heaven or hell. Consequently CCR recommends caution in comments implying anything in regard to such. For example, it is unclear what impact a person's material aspects (such as hunger, a brain tumor, or upset stomach) may have on that person's spiritual aspect although it is evident such can impact a person's thinking and behavior.

The above statement about God goes beyond what many within Christendom profess or appear to believe by their words and actions. The God described above is greater than what seems to be their concept of God. The God described above is the kind of God Who can do the impossibility of something harder than a camel going through the eye of a needle (i.e., get a human, whether a good rich man or a poor miserable slob, into heaven). The God described above is the kind of God Who can take care of His follower who in response to God's words in Scripture and guidance from the Holy Spirit does things that do not make sense financially (such as a Jew in the Old Testament obeying the Mosaic Law in regard to loans to fellow Hebrews shortly before the time all loans are to be forgiven).

Believing that God is truly the God revealed by the Scripture is the foundation upon which the spiritual unity Jesus desires for His followers rests. CCR contends that such unity facilitates the powerful working of God through His church. Certainly appreciation for and understanding of the nature of God noted above is what enables the follower of Jesus to give thanks continually and to constantly be in prayer (communicating with the loving Father).

Selected Scriptural support for the above comments is presented below. As an initial exposure to CCR, this book does not provide the kind of comprehensive support for the tenets that would be characteristic of a systematic theology; such is likely to be done by other publications about CCR.

- God is the creator of all: Genesis 1 and John 1. And He is eternal: Revelation 4:8
- God sustains all: Colossians 1:16-17 and Hebrews 1:3.
- God is omniscient: Psalm 139:1-12.
- There is one God: Exodus 20 and Matthew 22:35-40.
- Jesus claims He and the Father are One: John 17. Jesus gives the Holy Spirit divine billing in Matthew 28:19.
- God is holy and loving: John 3 and Ephesians 2.

The above presentation of CCR beliefs about God has not delved into perichoresis (the subject of relationships among the three Persons of the Godhead). That topic was not a focus of the early church, but later (in the fourth and following centuries) got a lot of attention. This book will not dive into that whirlpool; instead this book simply affirms every statement the Scripture makes about the persons of the Godhead and warn against expanding those statements in ways that do not fully accommodate everything else the Scripture says about God.

4.3.2. God's Plan of Salvation

The Scripture is clear: the sin nature of humanity since the fall by Adam and Eve in the Garden of Eden has prevented any one (except Jesus) from living a life that satisfied God's standard of perfection. That standard of perfection is simply stated in what Jesus says in Matthew 22 is the first and most important commandment: to love God totally (with all the heart, soul, and mind) all the time (implied). Few would dare claim to have done that for a day or even an hour; too many other things pull at a person's heart, soul, and mind for God to be at its center so completely for very long.

Hence salvation by human righteousness (i.e., works) is as impossible as for a camel to go through the eye of a needle. God's plan of salvation involves payment for the guilt of sin by the death of Jesus the Christ and then an offer of salvation to people on the basis of God's grace. A person receives that salvation by faith, trusting God to keep His promise of forgiveness and eternal life to those who accept in trust what Jesus did for them as acceptable to God. God's plan of salvation involves both God and the person. God in His omniscience and sovereignty knew and decided who would be saved from before creation and the person must decide to accept God's offer of salvation in Christ. How these two aspects fit together without compromising one or the other is beyond human capacity to understand fully or to explain fully in finite conceptions, but the two things do fit together and CCR accepts both aspects of salvation as fully true, as presented in the Scripture. Romans 1-8 is the most thorough explanation of God's plan of salvation in the Scripture; the same basic perspective is presented in the book of Hebrews. The essence of God's plan of salvation is also found in John 3.

CCR recognizes that some people may fool themselves as well as others about their relationship to God, mouthing words of faith in Christ but ultimately trusting their works or their church to be what really saves them; perhaps such people will even appear to be spiritually powerful. This is probably the situation with those Jesus describes in Matthew 7:21-23. Some people may be unsure of their salvation, although the Scripture clearly states that once God truly saves a person that person stays saved because God holds on to the person securely.

CCR recognizes that if a person's life fails to give indications of a living relationship with Jesus by love for other believers in Jesus, the fruit of the Spirit, and obedience to Christ's commandments, the person should not have confidence in his or her salvation but should check to ensure that he or she is truly connected to Jesus.

God's plan of salvation is a topic where followers of Jesus often divide. Some even claim that a person has to not only accept a particular perception, but must also be part of a specific religious organization (i.e., church) to be saved. Some so emphasize one aspect of the truths stated above that other aspects are neglected or distorted. For example, before William Carey left England as a missionary to India in 1793, he had to convince his fellow Particular Baptists that missionary endeavors to evangelize were appropriate because their hyper-Calvinistic beliefs discouraged missionary endeavors. Carey did that with publication of his 1792 groundbreaking missionary manifesto, *An Enquiry into the Obligations of Christians to use Means for the Conversion of the Heathens*. CCR urges all to accept fully all the Scripture says about God's plan of salvation and not so emphasize just part of it that other parts are not fully accepted.

4.3.2.1. Exclusiveness of God's Plan of Salvation

The Scripture is very clear. There is no salvation apart from Jesus Christ. The Apostle Peter states this very clearly when he and the Apostle John were brought before the Jewish leadership (the rulers, elders, scribes, the high priest, and all of the high-priestly family) by the temple guards, having been taken into custody the evening before, to explain why they had been in Solomon's portico (a colonnade with double columns run-ning along the eastern wall in the Court of the Gentiles of Herod's temple) teaching the people that Jesus had risen from the dead (the Scripture says thousands who heard them believed). Peter is quite explicit. He said there is no salvation apart from Jesus and no other name by which people could be saved (Acts 4:12).

The message of this kind of exclusive salvation is presented throughout the book of Acts in messages given in Judea and in the messages reported from the missionary journeys in Turkey and Greece. It is also the mes-sage clearly explained in the Apostle Paul's explanation of God's plan of salvation in the book of Romans.

Such exclusiveness is anathema to many in contemporary America because it reflects commitment to a truth they deny. Tolerance is their mantra, and to them tolerance is more than respect for a person with a different opinion. Some tolerance advocates promote an exaggerated perversion of tolerance which basically accepts all (or at least many) religious claims as equally valid in their ideas about God and how one is acceptable to Him; such a view implies there is no such thing as truth about God. Some who have such major emphasis on tolerance and inclu-sion of all sometime contend that such should apply not just to "reli-gious" beliefs but also to social attitudes and castigate those who cite the Scriptural teaching that homosexuality is sinful (even though it basically has become legally acceptable in America today).

Some seem to think diversity of religious belief and practice is a new phenomenon that Christianity is encountering. It is not a new or recent situation. America started with religious diversity: the variety of religions practiced by Native Americans (which typically have been ignored in discussions of religious diversity in America, especially on the North American continent), Catholicism from Spanish and Portuguese explorers, and a plethora of Protestant groups from European setters. In the late-19th and during the 20th centuries, immigrants from the Orient (both the Near East and the Far East) brought a variety of religious expressions with them which increased the religious diversity of American society.

Some prefer to discuss the variety of religious expression in America under the label "plurality" instead of diversity (e.g., the Plurality Project at Harvard University which began in the 1990s). Often the philosophical approaches of those who reject "religious" ideas (such as communism and secular humanism) are treated as quasi-religious groups in discussions of diversity or plurality.

Christianity began in a world (basically the Roman Empire of the first century) with as much and perhaps even more religious diversity than exists in contemporary America. In addition to Judaism and Christianity, the Romans, the Greeks, and the Egyptians each had a collection of deities, and some localities added others. Typically the authorities favored one or more of the local religions, and most were hostile to Christianity. Sometimes there was even Empire-wide (or at least regional) persecution of Christians by the Roman authorities. It is also true that often those with political power did not tolerate ideas (including religious beliefs) at odds with those of the rulers; unfortunately "Christian" authorities have done that as have others (to the dismay of all followers of Christ who try to comply with Scriptural instruction).

Christian Scripture is very clear: only those who trust in Jesus for salvation can escape the eternal consequences of their sinfulness. It is not intolerance to warn others of the danger they face if Jesus is not their Savior. Such warnings can be given with respect for the individual's right to believe as he or she chooses. Those who call the belief that salvation is only possible through Christ an expression of intolerance (as some do) show a lack of concern about the truth.

4.3.3. Christian Scripture

Christian Scripture is the source of reliable information about God that is generally applicable to all people of all time, but the topic of Scripture itself should not be primary in one's beliefs. God and His plan of salvation should be primary. This was illustrated by the early church. That behavior of the early church (keeping God and His plan of salvation primary) was part of the reason God worked so powerfully through the early church, expanding those following Jesus Christ from a small group of Jews in the Roman Province of Syria to a significant portion of the population of the whole Roman Empire (plus others). Unfortunately some within Christendom fail to comprehend this, and have made beliefs about Scripture primary. This is illustrated by what comes first in the statements of faith and confessions for a number of groups within Christendom: it is a statement about Scripture.

For example, a statement about Scripture comes before a statement about God in the statements of faith of the following groups in modern America:

- National Association of Evangelicals (NAE) which began in 1942 and is associated with about 40 different denominations;
- the Independent Fundamental Churches of America (IFCA) established in the 1930s;
- the *2000 Baptist Faith and Message* from the largest Protestant denomination in the United States; and
- statements of faith for various Pentecostal denominations, the Assemblies of God, and many dispensationalists as reflected by statements of faith from Bible colleges.

Putting Scripture before God in past statements of faith occurs in the 1536 A.D. *Geneva Confession of Faith* which reflects the teachings of John Calvin and in the 1646 A.D. *Westminster Confession of Faith* which played a significant role in English-speaking Christianity and especially among Presbyterians. However, such puts these confessions of faith at odds with other expressions of faith that appear in the Reformed segment of the Protestant Reformation.

Placing Scripture before God in such statements of faith contrasts with what was put first in the earliest creeds of Christendom with widespread acceptance: The Apostles' Creed and The Nicene Creed (God was the first topic addressed). It also contrasts with what comes first in a number of confessions of faith early in the Protestant Reformation: they address the Godhead before addressing Scripture.

For example, the first article of the 1530 A.D. *Augsburg Confession* which was the primary confession of faith of the Lutheran Church deals with God. The *39 Articles of the Anglican Church* from about 1570 A.D. also address God in the first article as does the 1790s A.D. *Articles of Religion of the Methodist Church*. The 1619 A.D. *Belgic Confession* is one of the oldest doctrinal standards of the Reformed branch of the Protestant Reformation; its first statement addresses God. In a precursor to the Protestant Reformation that began with Martin Luther, the 1120 A.D. *Waldensian Confessions of Faith* address God before the Scripture.

It is recognized that statements of faith, confessions, and creeds often have multiple purposes. They not only present a summary of basic beliefs, but they also often emphasize things that may distinguish that group from other groups. Such distinctive aspects of an expression of belief may deal with fundamental beliefs such as God's triune nature or eternal security of salvation, particular church practices such as acceptable modes of baptism or a specific connotation for aspects of communion (e.g., consubstantiation), details of eschatology, etc. Consequently prevailing circumstances when a creed, confession, or statement of faith was developed may influence the order in which topics are addressed so that items of greatest interest at the time show up first, and their order of appearance may not necessarily indicate the true relative importance of the topics for the group producing that statement of faith. It is necessary to keep this in mind for proper perspective about the comments above.

The discussion thus far has been about possible improper priority in doctrine, i.e., putting another topic (such as the Scripture) higher in priority than the primary topics of God and His plan of salvation. This discussion has not yet begun to address the character of Scripture. Now the Scripture and its characteristics will be addressed.

Because CCR takes the Scripture seriously, CCR deals with the Scripture as it is. This means CCR deals with the reality of the Scripture as it exists today. That reality is addressed honestly with candor, and is not distorted by imposing upon the Scripture an ideology not clearly taught by the Scripture itself. This is hard to do because humans have a tendency to make things more complete so they package more neatly logically, and then give to the tacit assumptions in doing that the same authority as given to the actual statements of Scripture.

Unfortunately taking the Scripture seriously as CCR does can put CCR at odds with some godly people whose beliefs have gone beyond what the Scripture actually says and with the reality of Scripture today. In spite of that, CCR is convinced it is always wisest to take the Scripture seriously; and thus presents the perspective described below.

4.3.3.1. The Autographs

The Scripture is authoritative because it is from God (written by people inspired by Him) to reveal God and His plan of salvation to people (2 Timothy 3:15-17; Hebrews 1:1-2 & 4:12). As the inspired Word of God in written form, the autographs were true without any error (this is an assertion: such is not explicitly stated in Scripture – nowhere does the Scripture explicitly say that no untrue item, such as a misspelled word or incorrect date, existed in an autograph of Scriptural writing), and such perfection cannot be claimed for any extant copy since its exact relationship to the autograph is unknown.

Typically confessions and statements of faith which put discussion of Scripture ahead of discussion of God identify Scripture passages supporting their position (e.g., *2000 Baptist Faith and Message*); some (e.g., *Westminster Confession of Faith*) even specifically identify which specific writings are considered Scripture and some that are specifically noted as not being Scripture. Earlier CCR identified which writings are considered undisputed Scripture as the source for "clear teachings" from Scripture, but left identification as Scripture or non-Scripture of the disputed writings unsettled. Inclusion or exclusion of the disputed writings will not contradict the "clear teachings" of Scripture noted although they may add secondary things to them. An example of such a secondary thing is the name of an angel, Raphael, which is found in *Tobit*, a book of the *Apocrypha*.

The way that a secondary doctrine such as one about Scripture can be elevated is illustrated by the 1978 *Chicago Statement on Biblical Inerrancy* (accessed at http://www.alliancenet.org/the-chicago-statement-on-biblical-inerrancy in August 2017). This statement was prepared by a number of noted Biblical scholars. The following are items 4 & 5 in what is called "A Short Statement."

"4. Being wholly and verbally God-given, Scripture is without error or fault in all its teaching, no less in what it states about God's acts in creation, about the events of world history, and about its own literary origins under God, than in its witness to God's saving grace in individual lives.

5. The authority of Scripture is inescapably impaired if this total divine inerrancy is in any way limited or disregarded, or made relative to a view of truth contrary to the Bible's own; and such lapses bring serious loss to both the individual and the Church."

It is hard to square these words with the experience of the early church, a portion of church history that demonstrated God's working through it in remarkable ways. It was also a portion of church history in which some Christian writers (or their parents or grandparents) had been instructed personally by the apostles of the New Testament. In addition, it should be noted that such emphasis on inerrancy seems to have created unnecessary divisions within Christendom, and that may have hindered God's work through contemporary Christendom as much as the possible harm from "serious loss" mentioned in item 5 above.

4.3.3.2. Scripture Available Today

People have a tendency to go beyond the evidence, as was noted earlier about scientific claims. It is also a problem in religious circles. It is easy to find such statements, even from noted scholars. Sometimes such statements present a more complete or more consistent perspective than provided by what the Scripture actually says. This is illustrated by Article X in the 1978 *Chicago Statement on Biblical Inerrancy*. It states that "inspiration, strictly speaking, applies only to the autographic text of Scripture, which in the providence of God can be ascertained from available manuscripts with great accuracy."

No one has ever checked the correctness of this statement about "great accuracy" by comparing anything extant today with a copy of one of the autographs because none of the autographs are available today. The statement quoted is an expression of hope. No Scripture passage promises that a reliable copy of any portion of Scripture will always be available or if it were how it could be identified as such. It is a comforting thought that God somehow made a reliable copy of His Word available, and this statement uses the term "providence of God" to enshrine that thought with religious authority; but the Scripture itself does not say such.

Think through implications of the assertion made in Article X. It suggests that somewhere there has been a replication of autograph content with great accuracy. Lack of awareness of *ALL* New Testament books by any second century Christian writer raises the question of what that assertion means. Did it only mean that some place in the world at any time there was a copy of every bit of Scripture with great accuracy? Or did it only mean that at some point later in history, manipulation of extant materials would allow a copy to be developed with great accuracy? Even a short period of hard and clear thought identifies a number of issues with the excessive claim asserted by Article X.[52]

Difficulty exists in sorting more reliable information from less reliable information, such as textual criticism has to do in deciding which manuscript variant should get priority. A similar kind of problem often exists in dealing with data from tests, such as tests to determine what happens to an underground facility exposed to explosive forces. The same parameter (such as the level of shock at a particular point or the extent of damage to a corridor or room) may be measured by different kinds of instruments (optical ones, RF ones like radar, or physical measurements after a test) or even by the same kinds of sensors in different locations (such as some sensors in front of the test object and other sensors behind the test object, or off to the side of the test object). Often results vary significantly from the different sensors. Different analysts addressing data from a test will consider different sensors as the most reliable, and sometimes it is very hard to tell which sensor is more likely to have the most correct information. Similar uncertainties and difficulties exist in textual criticism; reliable information about the provenance of a manuscript may be limited or suspect.

Assumptions about the reliability of extant Biblical materials (a topic which Scripture itself makes no direct comment about) should be considered very carefully, especially statements such as that quoted from the *Chicago Statement on Biblical Inerrancy*. Such caution is needed when such statements come from reputable and respected scholars well-known for their dedication to Christ (as is the situation of the material quoted from Article X).

There is a human tendency to embellish things, even important things and not just the size of a fish that got away as stated by a fisherman. This is illustrated by the printed Greek versions of the New Testament that in 1633 A.D., a century after first publication of a printed Greek New Testament was given the title "Textus Receptus" as an advertising gimmick by the publishers to promote sales. The first edition of the Greek New Testament by Erasmus in 1516 A.D. included numerous verses not from Greek manuscripts but translated into Greek by Erasmus from the Latin Vulgate. He also changed the exact reading of the Greek in a number of passages so it read as Erasmus thought it should instead of how it was in the Greek manuscript he was using. It is only in Erasmus' third edition in 1522 A.D. that he added material in 1 John 5:7-8 from the Latin Vulgate (the official Bible of the Roman Catholic Church) to avoid criticism; Erasmus had not found that material in any of the Greek manuscripts he had seen. Those copying Scriptural manuscripts in antiquity may have behaved at times like Erasmus. What that would mean for the accuracy of a particular copy is impossible to determine at this time; it could make the copy more like the autograph or it could make the copy less like the autograph.

The Scripture is written in normal human language and should be approached with recognition of the characteristics of normal human language. Words have meaning; sometimes they have multiple meanings and may not always be properly understood by those for whom they are intended. Language is both absolute (literal) and figurative (which includes exaggeration, sarcasm, irony, and other figures of speech). Passage meaning is impacted by its context (who speaks, to whom, for what purpose, when, where, in what situation, etc.).

Because the ultimate author of the Scripture is God Himself, Scripture often helps to understand Scripture and to put the full significance of a passage into proper context; this is especially important when *sensus plenior* may have pertinence relative to the passage. God's revelation of Himself and His plan of salvation is progressive; not everything was revealed at one time. The clearest indication of this comes from the new covenant's replacement of the old covenant (as described in Hebrews). The Scripture itself never claims that there will be no additional Scripture. The church historically has just assumed that there would be no additional Scripture after the New Testament apostles and their immediate associates had passed on ("associates" was included to accommodate the unknown author of Hebrews). That assumption provides an easy way to reject things such as the books that Mormons suggest are additions to the Christian Scripture; but the assumption has no explicit basis in Scripture.

This book does not claim there has been no revelation from God since the last book of the New Testament was written. CCR only says that any such revelation will not be considered undisputed Scripture and used to establish clear teachings.

CCR claims that it approaches reality with honesty and candor; that it admits both the certainties and uncertainties it encounters in reality, whether in the spiritual realm or in the material realm. Not everyone within Christendom (or in secular society) does that. Consequently there will be disagreement with some of CCR's perspectives by others. CCR tries to approach all issues calmly, courteously, and emphasize reality. It is hoped that others will do the same. When such occurs, it is possible that dialogue about areas of disagreement can lead to a more correct understanding of that aspect of reality. Whether that will occur or not for topics where the CCR view is different from that of others remains to be seen.

To illustrate this issue, consider the warning from Scripture not to add to or take away from the Word of God (Deuteronomy 4:2 & 12:32; Revelation 22:18).[53] That seems to be a clear warning not to distort God's Word by changing it with addition to it or removal from it. How would such apply to Matthew 6:13 and 1 John 5:7. The traditional texts of these two verses have material that textual criticism says were not part of the original Scriptural texts, but were added later. Various reasons have been suggested for the additional materials. Who errs? The one accepting the traditional reading because it probably has been added to the Word of God? Or the one who accepts the shorter version because it removed something from the traditional text?

This simple example shows why calm, factually oriented discussion is needed because even simple issues such as this example can trigger strong emotions and people sometimes respond in such situations with hasty and hostile words, unkind feelings and comments, and wrong motivations. Such behavior does no one any good.

God's power to work through His church and to use His Word is not dependent upon puny human efforts to defend or protect His Word. It is better to trust Him, and not make claims that go beyond what He has said in the Scripture. That goes against the human tendency to make things more complete or stronger, but it is a wise way to behave.

This discussion has shown why one should be cautious about what some say about extant Scriptural materials. What is the bottom line on this? What does CCR say about extant Scriptural materials? The CCR position on the autographs was clearly stated. The CCR position about extant Scriptural materials is recognized as an assumption (an uncertainty); it is not a Scriptural doctrine since (as noted earlier) the Scripture does not address this subject. The extant materials provide a basis for Scripture that reveals God and His plan of salvation. The average person can use any major translation of the Scripture to learn about God and His plan of salvation.

This comment does not claim the kind of inerrancy for any version of the Bible that was noted in material quoted earlier; and the CCR position above does not imply that all versions (texts and translations) of Scripture are equally reliable (some are better than others). Appropriateness of this perspective is illustrated by an experience of the author years ago in the Henrico County Jail in Virginia.

One of the inmates was a Jehovah's Witness. He refused to participate in the worship services, Bible classes, Christian films, etc. that the ministry in that jail provided. He even refused to talk with the chaplain or others about religious topics. One day, the chaplain surprised him by asking if they could have a discussion about things his version of the Bible said. He agreed. So the chaplain met with him in his cell; in that jail, the chaplain often went inside the cell blocks and talked with men in their individual cells because the jail, a Civil War era building, had no place for private discussions. They took the inmate's Bible, a copy of the New World translation, and began to look at what is called the "Romans Road."[54] God's plan of salvation comes through just as clearly from those verses in the New World translation as it does in the major translations used by most people. The man was stunned. He realized that his Bible said the same thing as he had heard the chaplain and others in the Christian programs at the jail say. He said he needed to think about things. Unfortunately he left the jail before he and the chaplain had a chance for additional discussion; it is unknown whether or not he acted on insights he got from the verses of the Roman Road.

This experience shows that God can reveal Himself and His plan of salvation even through Bible versions that many criticize, and which may not be based upon the best available manuscripts or translated the most accurately. Hence, the CCR position stated above. Of course, a religious writing called Scripture can be distorted so badly that it may not properly reveal God's truth, such as the notorious Bible of Thomas Jefferson that deleted all the miracles of Jesus (including His resurrection).

4.3.3.3. Excessive Claims for Scripture

Exaggeration is common. It is expected from fishermen about the one that got away. Exaggeration occurs in scientific claims as well as in mundane areas of life. And exaggeration also exists within religion. Some exaggerations relative to Scripture (such as applying things the Scripture says about its original documents, the autographs, to extant Scriptural materials) already have been discussed. Instead a few exaggerations in the teachings of some who claim such is based in Christian Scripture are discussed here; such exaggeration stands in marked contrast to the honest and candid approach to reality (including Scripture) that CCR advocates. Unfortunately that kind of honest and candid dealing with reality often is not done by proponents of various religions (it is not just a problem of Christianity) as well as by some secular approaches to reality.

As a youth in Baptist-dominated Dallas in mid-20th century, the author mainly associated with those who worshipped in Baptist churches; and he was exposed to various exaggerations of Scriptural truth. For example, Scriptural condemnation of drunkenness (e.g., Ephesians 5:18; 1 Peter 4:3) was exaggerated into prohibition of any drinking of alcoholic beverages. Some of the people he knew as a teenager were active in Pentecostal churches which had exaggerated Scriptural instructions about modesty and personal behavior (such as found in 1 Peter 3:2-5) into prohibition of lipstick, cosmetics, and most jewelry for ladies. Women who were regular participants in such churches were easy to identify visually.

In addition to exaggeration of a particular doctrine from valid Scriptural guidance about something into an excessive prohibition or command (as illustrated by the two examples above), there is another kind of exaggeration that one encounters; it perhaps is more pernicious and difficult to deal with. It is the idea that the Scripture provides guidance about every aspect of human life and provides all a person needs to know to deal with anything one encounters in life.

There are many things that the Scripture does not address. One of them is political structure. In the Old Testament, God gave the Jewish people guidance about their political structure since they were to be the people through which God would bring the Messiah (the Christ). However, in the New Testament there are no instructions for the church (God's people, Jew and Gentile, who follow Jesus) about political structures; there is only instruction to obey and pray for the political authorities. Hence the Scripture does not present a preference for democracy, a republic, a constitution, a monarchy, or something else. Likewise it is hard to find guidance in the Scripture about many decisions that face business leaders (such as a Scriptural attitude about unions, automation, minimum wage requirements, business records, etc.). Thus those who suggest that "every major and significant life area is addressed in the Bible"[55] have expressed an exaggeration.

Certainly the Scripture gives guidance that applies to people all the time, and Christians who seek to please God will strive to live accordingly to such, wherever those people may be in life. If that is what people mean by the quote above, they are correct. However, if they mean something more, as some do, then they exaggerate the Scripture. Beware of this kind of Scriptural exaggeration, and avoid it.

Some Christians seem to be afraid to deal with Scripture realistically, with honesty and candor. They seem to believe the Scripture needs to be protected and they make excessive claims about it, such as have been mentioned earlier in this section. God's Word does not need human protection. The Scripture can be presented as it is. That means acknowledging its uncertainties because the autographs are not available and it is impossible to specify exactly how any extant copy of Scripture came from the autograph of it. Likewise the Scripture does not need claims about it that it does not make for itself. Various statements of faith have divided believers and harmed the work of God by saying things beyond what the Scripture actually says and then insisting that all accept that statement of how things are. This has happened both in a variety of areas theologically and in regard to the Scripture itself. It's time for God's people to stop behaving so childishly.

4.3.4. People

This discussion is about human beings, people (old or young, of all sexes, of every race and ethnicity, and from all segments of society). For the past millennium, a primary connotation of the word "man" has been "a human being irrespective of sex or age."[56] However, currently that use of "man" to refer simply to a human being upsets some; so this section accommodates that contemporary attitude by discussing "people."

The Scripture says people have a sinful nature; and such prevents them from being able to satisfy God's standard of righteous behavior. Who can claim to have satisfied what Jesus said was the first or greatest commandment from God that is presented in the Scripture? Jesus quoted Deuteronomy 6:5 when He said, "You shall love the Lord your God with all your heart and with all your soul and with all your mind. This is the great and first commandment." (Matthew 22:37-38 ESV). Not stated explicitly, but implied is that this is to be done "all the time." Jesus then quotes from Leviticus 19:18 as the second greatest commandment: to love one's neighbor as one loves one's self. It is worth observing that a few verses later in Leviticus 19 it commands that one should also love the stranger living among them (i.e., aliens, people from other nations or of a different ethnicity) as one loves himself (verse 34). This too is something that human sin nature makes impossible for people to do perfectly. Jesus goes on to point out that all the law and the prophets of the Old Testament derive from these two commandments (Matthew 22:40).

In his epistle to the Romans, the Apostle Paul explains how the human sin nature that people inherit from Adam makes it impossible for people to meet God's standard of perfection; Paul then explains how God in His love for the world developed a plan of salvation based upon His grace made effective by a person's faith in the death and resurrection of Jesus to make forgiveness of sin and eternal spiritual life possible.

The Scripture notes that people were created in the image of God (e.g., Genesis 1:26-27), but does not explain exactly what that means. It must have something to do with people's capability to think, feel, trust, and love, but exactly what and how such may distinguish humans from other life forms is not clearly explained. It also seems that the image of God in people may be what allows those whose sins have been forgiven to be in Christ and have union with God. The letters of the New Testament draw clear distinctions between the relationship of lost people with God and the relationship of saved people with God (e.g., Ephesians 2:1-10). The lost are spiritually dead and alienated from God; the saved are alive spiritually and united with God in Christ.

The Scripture says a number of things about the way people behave, such as indicated by the advice for wise living provided in Proverbs. This book does not present such insights in a complete or organized way. It merely notes that such exists in the Scripture. Nor does this book try to provide a detailed description of human composition with its material and spiritual aspects. Previously comments were made about human responsibility (associated with the subject of free will) and findings of modern neuroscience. Such matters are not addressed here.

The Scripture presents a number of laws and insights for people related to wise and God-pleasing living. Some of these laws and insights are culturally dependent, such as dietary laws for Jews under the old covenant that specifically were discarded by the new covenant (Acts 11). Other insights continue to apply, such as the wrongfulness of murder, theft, false witness, and adultery. For some of the guidance, it is difficult to determine if such guidance was culturally dependent or if it has continuing and universal application. Guidance about sexual activities, such as things addressed in Leviticus 15, and gender restrictions in church activities are typically in this category. Detailed discussion of such issues is beyond the scope of this book.

Christian Scripture is a revelation so people can know Who God is, His plan of salvation for people, and how to live in ways that please Him. It is written in ordinary human language and accommodates to limitations of human comprehension. This is obviously true when Scripture addresses things that have complexities associated with reality's infinite aspects. It also seems to be true to some degree in comments about the beginning of things and some comments about material things, such as reference to the four corners of the earth several times (e.g., Ezekiel 7:2 and Isaiah 11:12) in various translations of the Scripture.[57] Christians committed to inspiration of Scripture have a variety of perspectives on such things, and this book does not try to walk through the issues involved. Instead this book simply posits that what God revealed in the Scripture is true and corresponds with reality when properly interpreted. That perspective also notes that current perspectives historically and scientifically may not correctly represent reality.[58]

Scripture indicates God holds people responsible for their behaviors and beliefs; CCR posits that how God evaluates them in this regard is always appropriate. God is righteous and makes no mistakes in anything He does. That does not mean that He always does things in the way that we, fallen humans, want or expect.

This is illustrated by Jesus in a parable about workers in a vineyard (Matthew 20:1-14). Jesus used the parable to teach about God's grace. All the workers were paid the same, whether they worked all day or just a small part of a day. This upset some of the workers, but as Jesus explained everyone was treated appropriately because each received what he had agreed to work for. Spiritually salvation is that kind of gracious treatment by God. The thief on the cross who turned to Christ shortly before his death went to heaven as did a person who accepted Christ as Savior at a young age and lived a Christian life faithfully for many years before dying.

4.3.5. The Church

Four connotations are attached to the word church. First, it is used to refer to a building where religious services are held. Although this connotation for "church" is frequently used today, that was never a Biblical connotation for the Greek word (ekklesia) that is normally translated "church" in the New Testament. When the New Testament was written (mainly in the second half of the first century), there were no buildings dedicated to Christian services or activities. The earliest example of a building dedicated to Christian activities appears in the third century, about 240 A.D. During the first century (the New Testament era), Christians met in private homes or public spaces (such as the temple courts, by a river, etc.). Sometimes Jewish Christians would talk of Jesus in a synagogue, but such might lead to expulsion of the Christians from the synagogue. Many meetings in private homes had to be small most of the time because there was not a lot of room in most homes. At most a few dozen people could be accommodated in most homes, and many could only accommodate a handful of people (this comment is based upon Paul's comment at the end of 1 Corinthians 1 which suggests that most Christians in the early church were not among the privileged of society since they included slaves and common folk).

However, if the home belonged to a well-to-do person, it could accommodate a large group. Over a hundred followers of Jesus apparently were together in a home when they selected the person to replace Judas as an official witness of the life and resurrection of Jesus (Acts 1). Jesus' first miracle, turning water into wine at a wedding festival in Cana described in John 2 apparently was someplace where a crowd could convene that might need over a hundred gallons of wine (the volume of water Jesus turned into wine).

Such well-to-do people apparently were available in many places. The Gospels suggest that a crowd often traveled with Jesus. That crowd almost always included a dozen-plus of His closest disciples. Apparently they were hosted when away from their homes. Several times banquets or feasts with Jesus present are mentioned in the Gospels; the implication is that they were sizeable gatherings. Hence the early church may have had both small congregations and sizeable ones.

The second connotation for "church" is a congregation; the believers who met together to worship, study, to serve one another, etc. This is the primary meaning of the Greek word (ekklesia) that normally is translated "church" in the New Testament. Sometimes the word "assembly" is used to translate the Greek word (ekklesia).

The third connotation for "church" is the collection of believers in a general area. This is what people normally mean when they refer to the "church at Corinth" or the "church at Ephesus." In this sense, the church at a particular location, such as Ephesus, would represent a number of congregations that meet for worship, education, and service.

For example, consider Ephesus in the early church. Hellenistic walls on the south-east side of the city were about 1.5 miles long. How far the area known as Ephesus extended in other directions is uncertain; but from the first century B.C. to the second century A.D., population of Ephesus was probably between 100,000 and 250,000; it was the second largest city of the Roman Empire in population. The temple of Diana was about 1.5 football fields long by 0.7 football field wide. A theater in Ephesus could seat about 25,000. In that kind of geography and population, a great many Christian congregations might exist in the church at Ephesus. Before the end of the early church (240 A.D.), there could have been more than 20,000 Christians in Ephesus if about 10% of the population had become Christians.

Some individual believers might participate in more than one congregation. How congregational leadership functioned in the first century is not known in detail. When a noted leader, such as one of the apostles or an elder, was in the area, did he interact mainly with just one of the congregations? Did he go from one congregation to another? Or did he only focus on interacting with leaders of the individual congregations? This latter approach was done at times. Acts 20:17-38 describes how the apostle Paul met with elders from the church of Ephesus[59] at Miletus as he was on his way to Jerusalem.

The fourth connotation for the word church is that of the universal church, the bride and body of Christ (1 Corinthians 12:27; Ephesians 4:12 & 5:22-33). This basically is the collection of all saved believers in Jesus in all locations from the birth of the church to the return of Christ. This connotation for the word church is addressed more fully in Section 4.3.5.1.

The fourth, fifth, and sixth CCR principles dominate this section. The Christian Scripture is taken as the reliable source of information about the spiritual aspects of reality; CCR considers the church as involved in the spiritual aspects of reality. The CCR focus on the clear teachings of undisputed Scripture, with such teachings addressed in multiple passages of Scripture, provides bounds on what God has to say about the church. Responsiveness to Christ's prayer in John 17 is addressed directly in Section 4.3.5.4. CCR uses information from writings of the early church to flesh out Scriptural teaching about the church.

4.3.5.1. Foundation and Nature of the Church

Here " church" is addressed in the fourth connotation for the word presented above. It is defined as "the collection of all saved believers in Jesus in all locations from the birth of the church to the return of Christ;" thus this definition includes both Christians now on earth and those who died and have gone on to be with the Lord. This connotation for the church is not held by all Christians. Some are not so definite about the beginning or ending of the church. They may mix redeemed from the Old Testament with believers in Jesus since the Day of Pentecost after His ascension, or they may include some saved during the Great Tribulation in the church.

Neither additional explanation of such beliefs nor argument about them is presented here; it is merely noted that some have a different view of the universal church than presented here for CCR.

Notice the two groups excluded by this definition of the church. Those who lived before the time of Christ that God has accepted are excluded. That means those God accepted such as Noah, Abraham, Job, Moses, Joshua, David, Elijah, Jeremiah, Isaiah, et al are not part of the church. They will be with God in heaven, but they are not part of the church. Likewise, those who turn to God after Christ returns and the church is raptured to be with Him are not part of the church. However, all who have accepted Jesus as Savior since the church began, whether alive now or who have gone to be with the Lord, are in the church.

Some carelessly assume everyone whom God considers acceptable to Him is part of the church, but that is not a view that seems fully consistent with what Scripture actually says. As the Apostle Paul makes very clear in Romans, all humans that God accepts as righteous receive their righteousness by God's grace through their faith. This was true of Abraham, the father of the faithful ones. It was true of the apostles of Jesus. It is true of every born-again believer in Jesus, and it will be true of those who are saved during the horrible time of the Great Tribulation. However, that does not mean all whom God accepts as righteous are part of the church.

The church has a specific and recognized beginning in Scripture. The first occurrence of the word "church" in the New Testament occurs in Matthew 16:18 when Jesus says He will build His church; these words suggest the church was not yet in existence. Jesus made that comment after Peter stated that Jesus was the Christ (God's promised anointed One, the Messiah), the Son of the living God.

This incident is the first time the Twelve reference Jesus as the Christ in the Gospels, but it is not the first time He was recognized as such in situations described in the Gospels. An angel told the shepherds the babe in the manger was the Messiah (the Christ) in Luke 2:11; later in that chapter Simeon recognized the child as the Christ (2:25-35). In Mark 8:29 demons recognize Him as the Christ, and Jesus confesses that He is the Christ to the Samaritan woman at the well (John 4).

God deals with those in the church differently than He dealt with people He accepted previously. Some aspects of His dealing with the church are presented as things which had been a secret (hidden, not revealed previously).[60] Primary among these mysteries is that Jews and Gentiles are treated the same in the church: "[4]When you read this, you can perceive my insight into the mystery of Christ, [5]which was not made known to the sons of men in other generations as it has now been revealed to his holy apostles and prophets by the Spirit. [6]This mystery is that the Gentiles are fellow heirs, members of the same body, and partakers of the promise in Christ Jesus through the gospel." (Ephesians 3:4-6 ESV). Galatians 3:27-28 makes the same point.

Another mystery concerns the Holy Spirit. The Holy Spirit was not described as being "in" the godly of the Old Testament as He is in those in the church and each believer is in Christ. The spiritual unity those in the church have is because they are the body of Christ; this too is also something different than the way God dealt with people in the Old Testament. Ephesians 1, Colossians 2, 1 Corinthians 6 & 12, and Galatians 3 are among the passages addressing the believer in Christ and the Spirit in them.

Usually the birth of the church (described in Acts 2) is stated as occurring on the Day of Pentecost, ten days after Jesus ascended into heaven as His disciples watched. There is good reason for recognizing such as the birth of the church. However, it was a while after that before the church was fully born. There were no Gentiles in the church (that we know about) until Acts 10 when Cornelius and his household learned of Jesus from Peter, believed and were baptized.[61] However that only demonstrated a partial expansion of the church beyond its initial Jewish constituency because Cornelius and his family were Gentile adherents to Judaism ("God-fearing" is the way the Scripture refers to them in Acts 10:2, the way Gentile adherents to Judaism were usually described). It was not until Acts 11:19ff that the birth of the church was completed when some of the Jewish followers of Christ from Cyprus and Cyrene began to tell Greeks in Antioch about Jesus and many of them become followers of Christ (so that the church truly was comprised of both Jews and Gentiles, as emphasized in the epistles of the New Testament). Then the term "Christians" began to be applied to those in Antioch who were followers of the Christ (Acts 11:26).

Jesus Christ is described as the builder of the church (Matthew 16:18), as its Savior, its head, and it being His body (Ephesians 5:22). The church is also described as His bride (Ephesians 5:29-32). Many associate the church with what Paul calls the "household of God" built upon the foundation of the apostles and prophets, with Christ Jesus as its cornerstone, and that whole structure being a holy temple in the Lord, a dwelling place for God by the Spirit (Ephesians 2:19-22). The manifold wisdom of God will be made known through the church (Ephesians 3:19). Similar comments about Christ and Him being the head of the church, His body are found in Colossians 1.

Since the church in this connotation is composed of a true Christians, it is appropriate here to mention some of the things that the New Testament says about true Christians, the ones that evangelicals would say have been born-again. The primary thing, especially as discussed in Ephesians but also addressed in other New Testament epistles, is that Christians are in Christ, sealed in His body by the Holy Spirit, and indwelt by the Holy Spirit as a guarantee of their eternal inheritance as children of God. As such, God sees them with the righteousness of Christ and has blessed them with every spiritual blessing. Being in Christ gives them immediate access at all times to God and assures them of His loving attention.

Obviously Christendom, the visible expression of those claiming to be followers of Christ (or at least those accepted in the community of religious organizations claiming some kind of allegiance to Christ), contains both true Christians (those that are saved by Christ who are in Him and the Holy Spirit is in them) and others. Eternal destiny of such others is unlikely to be heaven. They may be people like Jesus repudiated in Matthew 7:21-23 saying "He never knew them." Or they may be those labeled as Christian because of the geographic area where they were born, but never profess faith in Jesus; perhaps they may even explicitly deny that Jesus is God or the Savior.

Comments in this book focus on true Christians. Existence of others besides true Christians is recognized as part of reality, but this book does not give much attention to them. They like those with no attachment to Christianity need to come to know Jesus as their personal Savior. That is the most important thing they can do. And they would do it in the same way that everyone who knows Jesus as Savior has done. They would come to Him recognizing their need for salvation, acknowledging that they do not deserve such, but accepting by faith in Jesus God's gracious gift of forgiveness and eternal life. Romans 10:8-13 clearly explains what they would need to do.

It is simply noted that full discussion of the relationship between the church and God's people before Christ was born in Bethlehem and those alive after His return for the church are beyond the scope of this book.

4.3.5.2. Organization of the Church

The church which began at the Day of Pentecost, ten days after Jesus ascended into heaven as described in Acts 2, is built upon the foundation of the apostles and prophets, with Jesus Himself being its chief corner-stone (Ephesians 2:20). There was a group formally recognized as the official witnesses of what Jesus said and did while on earth. They were the Twelve, with Matthias as the replacement for Judas who had committed suicide, who had been with Jesus since the beginning of His public ministry (Acts 1). As the foundation for the church, the apostles helped to put what Jesus said into proper perspective. Two of them wrote Gospels (Matthew and John). Another (Peter) is thought to have been the primary source of information presented in Mark's Gospel. Peter and John also contributed five letters in the New Testament. Paul had contact with these men, as well as receiving revelation directly from God.

Prophets in the Scripture primarily present God's view on things (which some describe as "forth-telling"); prediction of future events (which some describe as "foretelling") is only a small part of what prophets say in the Scripture. With that perspective, one can see that the epistles of the New Testament are works of prophecy: they present God's view on God-pleasing living as well as God's guidance for the church. That contribution to the New Testament by the apostles and prophets largely provides the foundation for the church. Many fail to appreciate this primary role of prophets in Scripture because they focus mainly on prophecy as foretelling.

Revelation in Scripture is progressive[62]; that is illustrated in the history of the church, as found in the early chapters of Acts. Initially the church consisted of Jewish followers of Jesus, and it began in a spectacular way on the Day of Pentecost under the leadership of Peter (as described in Acts 2). Then when the church expanded to include Gentiles (as described in Acts 10), God used the same person (Peter) in a leadership role of the expansion and gave the same spectacular manifestations of His acceptance of the Gentile believers so that the church could understand that this expansion to include Gentiles with Jews in the church was of God.

During the early days of the church, when it was exclusively Jewish, there were no specified times of worship, no specified administrative structure, and no organization specified. This was in stark contrast with the extensive religious organizational structure in Judaism of the time.

Until the year 70 A.D. when the Romans destroyed Jerusalem, the focal point of Jewish worship was the temple in Jerusalem, where a hereditary priesthood offered sacrifices as described in the Old Testament. Jesus' family participated in such worship when He was a youngster (e.g., Luke 2:41-51).

The origin of synagogues is unknown, but synagogues were around and served as established community centers in the first century in Judea and Galilee as well as in the Diaspora. Synagogues were used as places for reading Scripture and worship or teaching (Luke 4:14-30), as schools (Josephus, *Antiquities* 16.43), for communal meals (Josephus, *Antiquities* 14.214-216), as hostels, as courts (Acts 22:19), as a place to collect and distribute charity (Matt 6:2), and for political meetings (Josephus, *Life* 276-289). First-century sources identify elders, priests, and *archisynagogoi* (Greek for "heads of synagogues") as leaders of synagogues.

The first indication of church organization came when issues arose about how alms were distributed, and a particular role was defined: deacon to administer distribution of assistance given to the needy. Establishment of deacons was to allow those who were the official witnesses of the life and teachings of Jesus, the Twelve with Matthias as the replacement for Judas, to devote themselves "to prayer and to the ministry of the word" (Acts6:4 ESV); they were recognized as leaders of the followers of Jesus. Other than believing in Jesus and being baptized as an indication of being His follower, nothing else was specified (at least as far as indicated by currently extant materials) for inclusion in the church, the community that accepted Jesus as the Messiah and worshipped Him as the Savior.[63]

A decade or two (perhaps even several) would pass before information about church organization and structure appears; that is when the epistles of the New Testament were written. When the epistles were written, the church had changed from a Jewish sect mainly in the Roman Province of Syria (which contained Judea, Samaria, and Galilee) into a religion that was mainly Gentile numerically and which was spread through much of modern Turkey and Greece, with collections of believers across north Africa, and elsewhere also (such as in Italy and to the east of Syria).

Epistles of the New Testament say that God gave the church people with capabilities to perform a variety of roles; the Apostle Paul mentions the following in 1 Corinthians 12:28: "first apostles, second prophets, third teachers, then miracles, then gifts of healing, helping, administrating, and various kinds of tongues." (ESV) Paul goes on to emphasize, as he does

97

elsewhere also, that doing God's work is a venture that involves many people, each doing different parts of the ministry, and that acting in love should always characterize what is being done. Elsewhere other spiritual gifts are mentioned, and Paul's perspectives on qualification for congregational leadership are presented in his letters to Timothy and Titus.

However, only general activities are specified in the New Testament epistles: to pray always, to give thanks in everything, to be a living sacrifice dedicated to Christ, to love others, etc. Nowhere in the New Testament are there specific directions about specified religious activities with designed times, identification of who should be involved as leader or participant, specified position for worshippers (such as kneeling), indication of relationships among roles, or words to be used in various religious activities. The closest thing to such specific directions in the New Testament is the admonition to communicate to other believers with psalms, hymns, and spiritual songs (Ephesians 5:19).

Such liturgical guidance as detailed structures for Christian meetings, specific words to be used in religious activities, etc. only begin to appear in the second century. An example of such liturgical guidance is found in *The Didache* (usually dated as originating in the second century). In addition to repeating various ethical behaviors from the Scripture, *The Didache* provides instruction about baptism, fasting, and communion; it specifies specific words to be used in prayer after communion. However, there is no indication such was part of church activities during the New Testament's formulation. One is hard pressed to present a credible claim that something is how things were done in churches of the New Testament era; there is too little specific information available from sources of that era.

Likewise, it is difficult to find any church today that is completely compatible with the New Testament. That comment may rile some feathers even though it is so obviously true. Most denominations and individual congregations have characteristics at odds with the New Testament. This is even true of churches which emphasize that their churches are "New Testament" churches. The church during the New Testament had to deal with such too. Judaizers wanted to add human accomplishments (such as circumcision) to faith in Christ as a required part of saving faith; that was addressed in both the Council of Jerusalem (Acts 15) and Paul's letter to the Galatians. Divisions based upon leader's personalities and particular teachings had to be addressed, as Paul did in his first letter to the church at Corinth. General warnings against false teachers and even false prophets and apostles are presented several times in the New Testament; and things said of them seem to characterize some within contemporary American Christendom.

For an example of incompatibility with the patterns of the New Testament church, consider the issue of baptism. The earliest specific reference to baptism of infants or young children is probably from about 180 A.D. in *Against Heresies* by Irenaeus (more than a century after Acts and epistles of the New Testament were written); most of the other early specific references to baptism of the very young come from the third century (or later). Baptism in the New Testament followed a person's faith in Christ for salvation; proponents for infant baptism note there is no prohibition against baptizing infants and claim that baptism of the very young was implied by references to the households of people being baptized (Acts 16:15, Acts 16:31–33, 1 Corinthians 1:16). Hence it is possible (if one restricts one's view to what is actually said and done in the New Testament) to characterize the way many groups baptize infants as out of keeping with New Testament guidance.

The association of baptism with a person's testimony to faith in Christ (a key function of Christian baptism) is indicated in the requirement to have a sponsor for the infant who would speak of faith in Christ in the child's behalf; such is specified in the *Apostolic Tradition*, a third century treatise about church activities, especially in Egypt that may have been written by Hippolytus of Rome, who died in 235 A.D.

Another example is presented here to illustrate how churches deviate from New Testament teachings. Many religious groups describe one of the leaders in the church by the term "priest." The priest in such churches is a person with privileges and authority that others in the church do not possess. Such is contrary to what one finds in the New Testament.

The New Testament has a specific word for priest (*ἱερεύς*, typically transliterated as hiereus). This word is used only of Jewish priests in the Gospels and Acts; in Hebrews it and priesthood refer to Old Testament priests and to Jesus or Melchizedek. Never is the word used to refer to a role that only some Christians may have in the church. A priest, in churches which have such, typically is an intermediary between God and people (as the priest was in ancient Judaism); the priest also is a person to present people to God in an acceptable way by offering sacrifices or conveying something to the people that makes them acceptable to God (this a perspective found both in churches with priests and in ancient Judaism). The New Testament says that is done by Jesus, not by any human agent.

Likewise the priest is expected to present God to people; the New Testament gives this responsibility to ALL believers in Jesus, as stated by the Apostle Peter in 1 Peter 2 where he talks about the universal priest-hood of ALL believers in Jesus. Hence religious groups that designate some Christians as "priests" with special privileges and responsibilities are at odds with the way the New Testament uses the term "priest."

Some religious groups who have "priests" as a person with a designated role of responsibility in the church that is different from the role and responsibility of all believers in Jesus try to justify their behavior by saying that the priest fulfills the responsibility designated for the "elder" (presbyter comes from the Greek word for elder) or "overseer/bishop" in New Testament terminology; but they identify responsibilities, roles, etc. for that position that are not part of what the New Testament says about the responsibilities of elders and overseers in the church. The leadership role of elders in Judaism was prominent, but was always distinct from the role of priests. Hence, the New Testament refers to "priests and elders" (in Matthew 26 & 27 and elsewhere).

This and the previous comments about infant baptism illustrate ways that some religious groups deviate from the New Testament pattern for the church. CCR seeks to be fully compliant with clear teachings from the New Testament. The New Testament says baptism follows faith in Christ and that all believers in Jesus are a holy priesthood that should present Christ to others by what they say and how they live. In addition, their lives should be a living sacrifice (Romans 12:1) in obedience to the Scripture and leading of the Holy Spirit in the person's life.

The two examples above of church practices that seem at odds with New Testament guidance about the church (i.e., priests and infant baptism) may encourage those in churches (such as most Baptist churches) that advertise themselves as an expression of New Testament Christianity to be proud they do not engage in such deviation from Scriptural guidance; but those groups should not be too proud since they also have practices at odds with New Testament teachings, as illustrated below by tithing.

Many such churches emphasize tithing as a "Christian standard," but it is not. The New Testament contains a number of passages about Christian use of financial resources. Paul was involved in collecting funds from a variety of churches to help poor Christians in Jerusalem. For example, specific guidance is given by 2 Corinthians 8:11-15, 1 John 3:17, and by James 1:27 regarding how a Christian should use financial resources; but never is it called "tithing."

In fact, the word "tithe" occurs only four times in the New Testament: once as part of a Pharisee's bragging in a parable (Luke 18:12) and three times in Hebrews 7 about Abraham's tithes to Melchizedek. The New Testament does not say Christians should tithe; it is not presented as a standard for Christians. Tithing is part of the old covenant that the New Testament in Hebrews 8 says has been put aside.

This book has made frequent reference to practices of the early church as useful examples to help contemporary Christians be more pleasing to God. It is appropriate to ask what is found in the early church practices relative to tithing. Clement of Rome (~100 A.D.) urged Christians to give their offerings systematically but makes no direct mention of tithing. *The Didache* (early second century) contains numerous references to giving but no reference to tithing. Justin Martyr (100-165 A.D.) in describing church services said to give as they saw fit. During the early church, nothing was said (directly) about tithing by Ignatius of Antioch, Polycarp of Smyrna, Quadratus, Tatian, Hippolytus, Kallistos, and Novatian. In the second century, Irenaeus apparently believed that Jesus abrogated tithing.[64] It was a century after the early church and Christianity had become politically acceptable to Roman authorities that the fourth century *Apostolic Constitutions* stated that tithes were "the command of God" and exhorted all Christians to give their first fruits and tithes.

Emphasis on tithing for Christians is another example of contemporary church deviation from the practice of the New Testament church.

Earlier it was said that most churches and denominations behaved at odds with the New Testament. The three examples mentioned (infant baptism, priests, and tithing) prove the truth of that comment since at least 80% of Christians in the world at present are in churches or denominations that practice or emphasize at least one of these three deviations from New Testament church teachings and patterns. It is quite possible that mentioning this topic will cause some to ignore everything else this book says and turn against CCR concepts.

Social privilege for the church as an organization and political acceptance of Christianity, especially of one particular expression of it, seems to have been spiritually detrimental most of the time. History is full of examples of the church in a position of political and social influence acting in very unloving ways toward those who do not kowtow to it. Typically church histories present a whitewashed version of what happened, accepting the dominant church perspective as historically accurate. One gets a very different perspective from a book like E. H. Broadbent's 1931 book, *The Pilgrim Church: Being Some Account of the Continuance of Churches Practicing the Principles Taught and Exemplified in the New Testament* (Pickering & Inglis, Ltd)[65] than one gets from most books of church history. In many situations, such as the Spanish Inquisition and the ways the Catholic Church in Medieval Times dealt with those who rejected its organizational authority (such as the Waldenses), the church acted as viciously and unlovingly as the Jewish leaders of the Maccabees reign did to Jews not adhering to Jewish tradition (they were killed, their possessions were confiscated, etc.). This kind of behavior was not restricted to the Catholic Church, but was also done by Protestant churches, as noted in the history of Protestants by Alec Ryrie, *Protestants* (Viking 2017).

4.3.5.3. Activities of the New Testament Church

Appreciation for the progressive character of Scriptural revelation dictates where reliable information about activities of the New Testament church is to be found. Since the four Gospels deal with events prior to birth of the church, they provide no direct information about activities of the church; nor do the early chapters of Acts since it is not until chapter 10 that God reveals to the early Jewish followers of Jesus in the church that Gentile believers in Jesus Christ will be included in the church with them.

Those early Jewish believers in Jesus seemed to have continued to have the Jewish perception that God was present in a unique and special way at the temple. Hence sacrifices and prayers there were more significant than sacrifices and prayers elsewhere; that may have been why Peter and John went up to the temple at the "hour of prayer" (Acts 3:1). Apparently God had not yet revealed, as is clearly stated in the epistles of the New Testament written two or three decades later, the full significance of what it means to be a member of the church: the essence of which is that the believer is in Christ. In Him, the believer has the kind of access to the presence of God at all times that previously only the high priest of Israel could have and that only once a year when he went into the Holy of Holies. In part this is why the new covenant makes no list of special days, special activities, and specific words for religious use since in Christ the believer has all that the privileged few had in the old covenant. The believer's life is to be a living sacrifice and a continual life of prayer (communication with God) and thanksgiving, as Paul notes in Ephesians 5 expressing itself to other believers in psalms, hymns, and spiritual songs.

The early Jewish church described in the early chapters of Acts deals with believers in Jerusalem and notes their involvement in the temple, their fellowship in meals, and sharing of possessions. The latter created problems. Desire for recognition led Ananias and Sapphira to lie to the congregation and experience the judgment of God (Acts 5); unequitable distribution of goods for the needy necessitated institution of a new role in the church, that of deacon to deal with that problem (Acts 6); and loss of income producing assets (such as property) from selling things to contribute to the common fund may have contributed to the church in Jerusalem being in such need later that help had to come for them from churches elsewhere.

The first use of the term "elder" in the New Testament for a role in the church appears to be in Acts 11:30 where "the elders" is used to refer to the leadership of the church in Jerusalem when the believers in Antioch decided to send alms to them by Barnabas and Saul (who is later mainly called by his Roman name, Paul). It could be that the Jewish Christians in Jerusalem had special need during the famine predicted by Agabus (Acts 11:28) because opposition from Jewish leadership to Christianity had cut the Jewish Christian needy in Jerusalem off from the normal means of distributing social assistance (which was through temple priests and the synagogues).

Epistles of the New Testament, especially those by Paul and Peter, suggest that Christians of the New Testament church met for worship, spiritual instruction, fellowship, and social assistance. No specific time or activities for such is stated; nor are frequency of meeting, location, mode of dress, etc. specified.

Twice in the New Testament (Acts 20:7 and 1 Corinthians 16:2) "the first day of the week" describes gathering of Christians. There are two issues. First issue, there is no indication that such was the only time Christians gathered, that this was the usual time Christians gathered, or that this was the pattern throughout the church since the two locations are in Greece and on the Turkish border near Greece. Patterns of Christian gathering across North Africa, in central Turkey, in the Roman Province of Syria, Italy, or the East may have been different. Second issue, it is not sure what "the first day of the week" may have meant in these Hellenized cities of Corinth and Troas since the phrase was used by a Gentile (Luke) writing for a Gentile friend (Theophilus). At this time in the Roman Empire, both the 8-day market week and the 7-day week of the Julian calendar were widely used. Each locality basically had its own calendar, and dealt with regular activities (such as market days, festivals, etc.) as it deemed appropriate. In Jewish dominated areas, the Hebrew 7-day week with the Sabbath (the 7th day) designated for worship/rest was used; so that in such conditions, "the first day of the week" would refer to Sunday (the day following the Sabbath) as it does in the Gospel accounts of the resurrection of Jesus (which were stated in terms of the Jewish culture of Jerusalem); or it could have been a different day (either based on the 8-day market week or however the locality set the 7-day Julian week). Reference to "the Lord's day" (Revelation 1:10) by John is variously interpreted as Sunday or a time related to the prophecy John received since he described himself as being "in the Spirit" at that time.

The first extensive description of a Christian meeting in extant Christian writings (about 150 A.D. in Justin Martyr's *First Apology*) occurs about a century after the New Testament epistles of Paul and Peter were written. Unfortunately, it is not known how the practice a century later related to what was done in churches where Peter or Paul ministered. It may have been very similar; or it could have been very different. Think about how many things have changed in churches in the past century. Once adult Sunday Schools were ubiquitous; now they are not. Once nearly all of a Catholic worship service was in Latin; now it is not. Once fire and brimstone sermons were heard from many pulpits; now they are not. Once most Protestant Sunday morning worship services started at 11 am; such is no longer the case.

The emphasis on the believer's position in Christ makes the Christian's life one in continuous intimate fellowship with God where one is to deal with all in a loving manner and to live in a God-pleasing manner at all times, exercising the spiritual gifts and natural abilities which God has given him or her, and encouraging and assisting others in their exercise of their spiritual gifts and natural abilities. This de-emphasizes a specified regimen of ritual and activities; as illustrated by the New Testament's silence in those areas. Relatively rigid liturgical practices came into prominence only long after the New Testament church and the early church; those practices became common after the church had gained political acceptance in the Roman Empire, especially after Christianity had become the official religion of the Roman Empire.

The church is both a spiritual and a social entity. During the early church, its essence as a spiritual entity presenting Christ as Savior and showing love for the followers of Jesus was dominant. In part, this occurred because the church little social benefits or political acceptance. Later as social benefits and political acceptance for churches became wide spread, the essence of the church seemed to be expressed by it being a social entity. Those involved in the church mainly because of geography (not because of personal commitment to Jesus) dominated the church socially (and politically). Any discussion of the church has to be conscious of both aspects of the church: it as a spiritual entity (which is what the New Testament focuses upon) and it as a social entity (which is largely what church history and history in general address).

4.3.5.4. Importance of Spiritual Unity

Just hours before He was arrested, Jesus prayed, "I do not ask for these only [His disciples, the apostles, who were with Him that night], but also for those who will believe in me through their word [all who have become followers of Jesus], [21] that they may all be one, just as you, Father, are in me, and I in you, that they also may be in us, so that the world may believe that you have sent me." (John 17:20-21 ESV)

God may work more powerfully through His people when they manifest spiritual unity than at other times. The Apostle Paul seems to have been acutely aware of this since he emphasizes the importance of spiritual unity in his epistles to the Colossians, to the Corinthians, to the Ephesians, to the Galatians, to the Philippians, and to the Romans. John and Peter also mention such in their epistles. The importance of such spiritual unity was understood by the early church. The Christian martyr, Ignatius of Antioch, urged spiritual unity in several of the letters he wrote to churches as he traveled to Rome for execution about 107 A.D.

Unfortunately contemporary Christendom seems to have lost sight of the importance of such spiritual unity, given its splintered condition and the unwillingness of many varieties of Christians to work with other varieties of Christians in evangelism, discipleship, or help for the needy. CCR provides a way for contemporary Christians to deal with this problem.

CCR suggests that individual Christians recognize the importance of being responsive to the prayer of Jesus for spiritual unity among His followers and that they follow the example of the early church in this regard. The early church emphasized the most important things (God and His plan of salvation) and did not allow other things (such as important but secondary doctrines, church tradition, personalities, etc.) to impede the spiritual unity Jesus sought for His followers. Thus, individual Christians can determine that they will be willing to cooperate with other followers of Jesus who share their commitment in faith to the God revealed in Christian Scripture and His plan of salvation in spreading the gospel of Jesus, encouraging people to grow in Christ (which is often called "discipleship"), and helping the needy. They can do this with (or without) the encouragement and assistance of leaders in their churches. Each Christian ultimately is responsible to God; this approach emphasizes that and places the onus on each individual Christian to be responsive personally to God.

Many past efforts to increase unity among Christians have focused on formal church organization and agreements; unfortunately, most such efforts have not been very successful in increasing spiritual unity among Christians (as demonstrated by the multitude of churches, denominations, and religious organizations which seldom demonstrate much spiritual unity with those in a different church, denomination, group, etc.). Whether or not the emphasis in this book on the attitude and behavior of the individual follower of Jesus will make a noticeable difference in spiritual unity of the church remains to be seen. Hope that it might drove this author to write this book and publish it. Of course, those in leadership positions within churches and Christian organizations also can do things organizationally and relative to agreements with others that they think will help promote unity among the followers of Jesus.

Some have noted that there are many connotations for spiritual unity. That is why the book includes Appendix B. It specifies what CCR means by spiritual unity that is responsive to the prayer of Jesus in John 17.

4.3.6. God-pleasing Living

For the Christian, a God-pleasing life is one in which Jesus Christ is Lord at all times. One's consciousness of what He has done to make our salvation possible and what it means to be saved (existing in Him and Him in the believer) encourages one to be a living sacrifice, obedient to guidance of the Holy Spirit in using (as a good steward) both the spiritual gifts and natural abilities with which God has equipped the person and serving Christ with others to evangelize, disciple, and edify. This makes one continually thankful and prayerful, allows manifestation of the fruit of the Spirit (love, joy, peace, patience, kindness, goodness, faithfulness, gentleness, self-control) essentially all the time, and shows Christ to others through the person's life as well as through the person's words.

The above description does not involve specific things that some have found helpful (e.g., feeding on the Word of God each day before nourishing oneself physically, or regular confession of one's sins, concerns, and anxieties to a fellow believer); nor does it involve a particular set of religious activities (such as regular attendance at worship services). However, it is believed that the above statement is a fair synopsis of guidance for Christians from the New Testament epistles. It avoids the one size fits all approach that many bring to guidance for Christian growth. The above recognizes that God deals with Christians as distinct individuals and equips each one for the particular things He has for that person to do as an individual; it also recognizes that God can change what He wants a person to be doing as that person lives in obedience to God's will.

Some might say that the emphasis of this section on the individual's personal relationship to Jesus misses the point of pleasing God in our time. They might argue that Christianity's role is to improve society by removing its evils of injustice, racism, intolerance, etc. They say what happens to society is what matters, not what happens with the individual. Some applaud secular progress in such, and lament that the church at times impedes such. However, CCR does not find the ideas, such as just mentioned, to be supported by clear teaching of Scripture, and therefore does not endorse them. This puts CCR at odds with some in modern society.

The Scripture is clear that God expects His people (at this point in time, the church, the followers of Jesus who reside in Him and He in them) to bless society as salt and light (in words from the Sermon on the Mount) as well as in the kind of godly lives indicated in the New Testament epistles. This book does not elaborate on what specifically that might mean in the lives of people today; instead this book deals with the issue more generally by addressing the follower of Jesus as an individual.

Scriptural support for the above comments comes primarily from the epistles of the New Testament.

Chapter 5.

CONCLUSIONS

CLASSIC CHRISTIAN REALISM (CCR) has potential to help contemporary Christendom have the kind of unity the early church had, and that may facilitate God's working more powerfully through the church than He has in the past century because the church will be more responsive to the prayer of Jesus in John 17. The splintered character of contemporary Christendom seems to limit God's work through the church.

CCR can help God's people have more spiritual unity without requiring administrative actions by groups (churches, denominations, religious organizations, etc.); such administrative actions are outside the realm of most Christians. The CCR approach only requires commitment from individual followers of Christ to emulate the early church in emphasizing the primary truth about God and His plan of salvation without permitting secondary things, even those doctrines considered to be very important or significant church traditions, to interfere with unity among believers in Jesus who are committed to the God revealed in the Scripture and to His plan of salvation. That kind of spiritual unity will manifest itself in many ways as the followers of Jesus respond to the leading of God's Spirit in their lives and demonstrate the spiritual unity that enables the world to believe that Jesus was sent by God the Father. Examples of such spiritual unity in Appendix B show the kinds of things that individual Christians can make happen.

It is hoped that many will take it upon themselves to share the perspective presented in this book with other followers of Jesus, and that God will work very powerfully through His people. It is possible that some will be so offended by comments about practices[66] found in contemporary

109

Christianity which seem to be at odds with terminology and teachings of the New Testament that they will simply ignore CCR; hopefully most reading this book will be wise enough to give CCR serious attention.

This chapter comments on several topics addressed in the book. These topics are: 1) Material Aspects of Reality, 2) Materialism and Secular Humanism, 3) Potential Corruption of the Church from Social Advantages and Political Acceptance, 4) Possible Reaction from Proponents of Biblical Inerrancy, and 5) What Lies Ahead for CCR? The chapter concludes with a few final comments by the author.

5.1. Material Aspects of Reality

CCR accepts as certainties laws of biology, chemistry, and physics that are based upon extensive direct observation (with appropriate explication of measurement conditions) for use in the earth environment with normal levels of radiation, gravitation, pressure, etc.; but that does not grant such certainty status to those laws for other situations (such as earth's past where radiation, gravitation, pressure, etc. may have been significantly different or for other places in our universe for the same reasons). Scientists can assume those laws might work in such situations as the past or other parts of the universe as long as they make it clear they are presenting speculation, and do not claim such to be fact.

Reluctance of scientists to be so candid is understandable since such candor about the uncertainties of what they do might impact the way their peers and their employers think of what they do. Such honesty and candor are likely to adversely impact a scientist's pocketbook, and those in science are as prone as everyone else to act in ways to protect their income (even if it requires a bit of deceptive behavior and less than complete honesty and candor).

This situation is illustrated by a number of important subjects that most researcher studiously avoid because one's career can be ruined by exploring such. Even notables such as recipients of the Nobel Prize have had their reputations savaged when suggesting ideas contrary to accepted perspectives in those areas. This reality seriously restricts candor in science. Those in the scientific and technical field are acutely aware of this situation; but it is not something that the general public understands.

The average person is not aware of how much modern science is merely speculation, not solid fact. The average person is not aware of the incompatibilities among widely accepted descriptions of reality, such as the Standard Model of particle physics, quantum theory, the Theory of Relativity, and however one wants to describe efforts to insert gravity into one's consideration of reality.

This author is not a scientist; but he was involved in technical aspects of society and associated with a number of scientists for decades.[67] So he has a reasonable basis for this perspective about how things are; these comments about material aspects of reality are consistent with perspectives of leading scientists. This perspective is illustrated by a quote from Richard A. Muller in his 2016 book, *The Physics of Time*. "As for understanding reality, it is time to recognize that physics is incomplete. Physicalism has been a powerful religion, very effective in advancing civilization by the focus it has given to physics, but not something that should be used to exclude truths that can't be quantified. There is reality beyond physics, beyond math."[68]

5.2. Materialism and Secular Humanism

Materialism and secular humanism so dominate education in America and Europe that the vast majority of their populations have grown up biased against honest dealing with the spiritual aspects of reality. The majority has been brainwashed so that they basically reject the idea that the Creator has provided guidance about wise ways for people to behave. Instead they emphasize tolerance and acceptances of all natural behaviors as acceptable.

People understand the importance of limitations on natural behavior in diet (otherwise people would be even more bloated than they have become because it is natural to want sweets and other things that are bad for people in excess), but similar acceptance of restrictions on natural behaviors sexually and in other areas (as recommended by Christian Scripture) are rejected out of hand because they are "just outdated religious traditions." It is time for the blinders to come off, and for the biased and deceptive nature of the approach to reality by materialism and secular humanism to be revealed. Perhaps such will help decent people immersed within secular humanism to wake up to what they are involved in.

The clear and explicit way that CCR addresses reality, both its spiritual aspects and its material aspects, should challenge those within materialism and secular humanism to think hard about their approach to reality.

Does their approach fully address all reality? Is their approach honest and candid with how it deals with reality? Many within materialism and secular humanism may not be happy with what they discover if they look at things honestly and candidly. Such might encourage some to consider the claims of Christ more carefully.

This book does not delve into conflicts between Christianity and science that are sometimes mentioned. Such conflicts (i.e., public exposure of different perspectives by respected representatives of various groups) have been given a great deal of attention in the past century or two. The topics mentioned at times include creation (when and how), age of the earth and things on it, a worldwide flood, development of humans by evolution or something else, historicity of various Biblical events, etc. This book, and its initial exposure to CCR, has not delved into any of these conflicts; instead the book (and CCR) focus on approaching every issue with honesty and candor, regardless of which aspect (scientific, Christian, or something else) one approaches the topic from. The certainties and uncertainties found in such an endeavor should be clearly distinguished, and each treated appropriately. This means that uncertainties (because they are mainly assumption based) should not be used to preclude other perspectives; only certainties should be allowed to do that. The main assumptions associated with a particular uncertainty should be made explicit. That will help people to determine how much credibility to attach to that uncertainty.

Unfortunately the history of religion, science, and philosophy shows vividly that such honesty and candor are seldom applied rigorously in any of the conflicts among different perspectives.

5.3. Potential Corruption of the Church from Social Advantages and Political Acceptance

History has shown how social advantage and political acceptance has corrupted the church repeatedly.[69] There are horrible examples of evil behaviors by the church when it used political influence to banish, persecute, and kill those who disagreed with it; unfortunately such evil behaviors are not confined to one or a few varieties of groups within Christendom. Even in its mildest forms, such as the "blue laws" in America,[70] exercise of political (legal) power by the church to force people to comply with its standards of behavior interferes with the Christian's primary mandate from Jesus to make disciples of all people. Christian discipleship must always be based upon a voluntary commitment to Jesus; not upon physical or other compulsion (or inducement) to do something.

Society is always challenged by the basis it uses to set its standards of behavior. For many centuries, a number of standards have claimed some kind of basis in Christianity (in some cases those claims were even true). For example, some laws (such as those against theft, murder, and falsehood in court) have a solid basis in Scripture; and some of those laws also have a basis in other systems of ethics too. Many Christians are very concerned when our laws clearly contradict Biblical guidance, such as laws making homosexual activities generally acceptable legally.

The early church provides one example of a way to act in such circumstances; Christians in the early church simply refused to worship idols or the emperor, and suffered for so doing but presented a witness of God's truth about such that put seeds in the minds and hearts of people that led to the salvation of some. They made no effort to gain control of the government and make laws according to what they thought was best. Some might choose that path today; and others might think it better to take a different approach.

One point is clear and undisputed: Christians should proclaim the truth revealed in God's Word. Not clear is what action is appropriate for Christians to take in shaping the laws where they live when circumstances (such as being in a democratic society) gives them opportunity to impact such laws. This book makes no attempt to provide general guidance about that complex issue.

In the past, some Christians have tolerated the evils of their society without rocking the boat. This seems to be what the Apostle Paul suggests in some of his epistles.[71] Other Christians have tried to thwart some evils by defying the government and breaking the law to help those being oppressed. This is what some did who helped former slaves fleeing on the "underground railroad" before the American Civil War, and what some did in Hitler's domain as they helped Jews avoid concentration camps.

Some Christians acted within the government to change what was being done. William Wilberforce is an example of such; his conversion to evangelical Christianity is recognized as a major factor in his successful efforts to end English involvement in the slave trade in the early years of the 19th century. God does not plan for all Christians to take the same approach in dealing with the ethical and moral issues of their time and situation; unfortunately, many Christians think everyone must accept the way that they see things in this area and adopt their approach or be condemned by them as doing wrong.

It is dangerous for Christians as a community (i.e., the church or other religious organization) to be too closely associated with government organizationally; that is likely to compromise the clarity and vigor with which Christians can proclaim the truth of God. Such compromise in its message is probably the least of potential corruption from social privilege and political acceptance the church (or other Christian organization) would experience. All varieties of governments are prone to evil behavior at times, as shown repeatedly by history. A church (or other Christian group) in bed with the government is likely to become involved in such evil behavior.

For example, Christian chaplains in the military are expected to pray for the success of military endeavors, at the individual soldier, sailor, or air person level as well as for operations as a whole. The American military at times has engaged in activities that at least in hindsight were not just or proper. What about the chaplains' prayers in those situations? What would happen had a chaplain refused to pray for or encourage success in an operation? This shows how connection between church and state can corrupt the church even in what are normally considered appropriate kinds of activities.

CCR restricts the period of the early church to the first two centuries of church history because that avoided most of the potential for corruption from social privilege and political acceptance that Christianity experienced later. That permits use of the early church as an example for dealing with the issue of spiritual unity before the pressures of cultural and political perspectives became as great as such are later in church history. This made the way the early church maintained its spiritual unity much clearer. That makes it easier for contemporary Christendom to emulate the early church in that regard.

A final comment about the potential dangers of social and political prominence for the church. The kind of situation described here appears repeatedly in church history. At times church leaders would behave like rascals to get their way and/or to elevate their positions within Christendom. This was illustrated in the 431 A.D. Council at Ephesus when Nestorius was condemned. Although Nestorius repeated proclaimed he believed that Jesus was truly God and truly man (which is consistent with what the Scripture actually says), because he did not accept the particular way that some in the church described the nature of the Son of God, the opponents of Nestorius forced the Council to act before representatives from churches in the East (which included churches in the Roman Province of Syria that contained Antioch, a center for Christianity since the days of the apostles) arrived so that the Council could condemn Nestorius and have him removed from the top spot in Constantinople (that allowed one of them to replace him). It was expected that those from the East would support Nestorius in this situation; which is why the Council acted before they arrived.[72] It is depressing to realize how many major decisions within church history were made in such disgraceful ways. It helps one to always emphasize looking directly to the Scripture for God's truth, and makes one very cautious about the reliability of church tradition as a valid spiritual guide. Too much of it reflect motivations that are not good.

We Christians are adapt at ignoring clear and explicit teachings of Jesus. In the Sermon on the Mount Jesus warns His disciples of the dangers of failing to show respect for others. He extends the prohibition against murder from the Mosaic Law to anger, insults, and calling one a fool (Matthew 5:21-22). Even the most casual reading of church history shows the great disregard for these words from Jesus in what Christian leaders say about those who did not agree with them. Those with dispensational inclinations may claim these words of Jesus apply to the Kingdom Age and are not applicable in the current Church Age; those with liberal tendencies may water down the consequences of behaving that way or explain things in some way that makes the words inapplicable to most people; and the rest are just likely to ignore what Jesus said. It is always wise to take Jesus seriously.

5.4. Possible Reaction from Proponents of Biblical Inerrancy

Some proponents of Biblical inerrancy may be unhappy with the perspective presented in this book, and possibly may even consider parts of it heretical. Certainly some comments in the book are incompatible with things in various statements of faith or other expressions of Christian belief. Proponents of Biblical inerrancy should have no problem with this book's comments about inerrancy of the autographs (although things in writings of some about Biblical inerrancy go beyond what the Scripture actually says); but no copies of the autographs currently are known to be extant and Scripture itself says nothing explicitly about copies such as are extant today. This book merely draws people's attention to that reality.

The points made and comments about the manuscripts are neither new nor previously unknown. All who are aware of information about textual history of the Bible have been exposed to these things. Some may dispute a fine point here or there, but most will admit that the general thrust of what this book says is consistent with the evidence. Unfortunately, some may permit doctrinal beliefs to cause them essentially to dismiss the historical evidence. The early church managed to be used powerfully by God while living with such uncertainties as noted in this book, and they maintained spiritual unity while doing it.

5.5. What Lies Ahead for CCR?

The future of CCR is up in the air. Its concepts need to be more fully developed and communicated. The author may be involved in some of that, but he would not expect to be the spearhead for that since he is too old and his personality is not one that would attract a strong following. Hence the future of CCR depends upon individuals sharing its concepts in hope that more spiritual unity will result and that God will raise up an appropriate person to be the spearhead for spreading the word about CCR.

Individuals can buy this book that lays out basic CCR ideas and then give copies of the book to pastors and others, encouraging them to give serious consideration to CCR ideas. Individuals can also commit themselves to the kind of spiritual unity described in this book; doing that will make them responsive to the prayer of Jesus in John 17.

It would be wonderful to see more unity among followers of Jesus. It would be great to see the followers of Jesus keep their priorities proper and not let secondary things separate them. It would be the greatest thing to see God work more powerfully through His church. Our world needs Jesus desperately.

Protestants, a 2017 book by Alec Ryrie (an expert on the Reformation in England and Scotland), which suggests that argumentativeness and divisions are primary traits of Protestantism, stimulates the question: is there any possibility of God working more powerfully through His church because a lot of individual Christians decide to be more responsive to the prayer of Jesus for spiritual unity? The answer to that question might be clear if CCR becomes widely known and a number of people become more responsive to Jesus' prayer.

5.6. Final Comments

In this section as in the Introduction, I use the first person informal style instead of the more formal way that the book is written. I thank all who read this book for the time and attention they have given to CCR. I appreciate comments that may correct factual mistakes and failures to properly attribute ideas to their originators. Such information provided to me by readers will be reflected in what appears in future communications. I do not claim to be the first to make any of the points found in this book. I have not deliberately failed to attribute important and distinctive ideas when I knew the originator. In general I have not identified specific people associated with ideas that I criticized because I do not want to possibly misrepresent another's views and because I want the reader to focus on the idea and how I address it rather than being for or against the idea because of its source.

I am fully responsible for this publication. I received helpful comments from about a score of people who reviewed preliminary versions of materials appearing here. I am very grateful for their comments, especially from three who reviewed the final version. One fact-checked scientific and technical comments, another checked for clarity of expression, and the third looked for typos. What I chose to do about comments I received was purely my decision and I accept full responsibility for what appears in this book. I have deliberately not named those who provided the helpful comments because I do not want any of them tarred by what may be a negative reaction to CCR since the comments by a particular individual may have had nothing to do with controversial matters. Also I am responsible for repetition in parts of the book. It is deliberate so that it will be less likely for information or logic holes to exist should sections of the book be extracted from the book as a whole. I apologize to all offended by seeing the same material more than once.

I thank God for Who He is, for His love for the world, and for His plan of salvation through Jesus. I appreciate the privilege that He has given me to share my thoughts with you through this book. I trust Him to guide you and you to respond to His guidance so that His will may be accomplished. I have tried to present CCR clearly and effectively; I hope you found it that way. May God graciously bless both you and me.

I confess that I had not recognized the importance that I believe spiritual unity among the followers of Christ has until a few years ago. I committed myself to Jesus as a youngster (at age 9 in a revival at a Baptist church, my parents did also, and the three of us were baptized at the same time). I was active in Southern Baptist churches in Dallas (Texas) from that time until I left for college a decade later. During those years of my youth except for involvement in a city-wide evangelistic campaign led by Billy Graham, my vision of Christianity was largely confined to what Baptists had done and were doing. I saw other churches and assumed they were Christians doing the same kinds of things my church did, but I had essentially no interactions with them religiously.

College, the Army, and seminary broadened my perspective about the scope of Christianity, but emphasis on doctrinal correctness (proper interpretation of the Bible) in my training caused me to erect barriers in my mind to those whose beliefs differed from my own. Even in my early years of ministry in jails and prisons, I focused on those with beliefs similar to my own and largely ignored churches whose theology differed from mine when I sought volunteers or financial support for ministry to prisoners. My thinking began to change a couple of decades ago.

Because inmates in jail are relatively transient (most states restrict the length of jail sentences to no more than a year or year and a half, longer sentences are served in prisons), ministry in jails can focus on the basics: salvation in Christ and the Christian Scripture as the guide to proper beliefs and godly living. Other aspects of doctrine can be emphasized when those from the jail are in churches in the community or in the religious programs within prison.

Ministry in jails can accept volunteers from churches of all sorts who are willing to focus on those basics and leave their denominationally distinctive beliefs outside the jail. I have seen how God has blessed that approach with much spiritual fruit over the years. Now I see that such an approach in dealing with the world was what allowed the early church to maintain its spiritual unity in spite of the different cultural backgrounds of its congregations. What I have seen happen in jail ministry shows that the ideas presented in this book are viable; they work.

In jail ministries I have seen people from AME, Assembly of God, Baptist, Episcopal, Lutheran, Methodist, and Presbyterian Churches as well as from independent and community churches, various Pentecostal groups, and other churches demonstrate that folks across the Protestant spectrum can work together in spiritual unity, spreading the gospel of Jesus and helping people, when focused on the basics of God, salvation in Christ, and the Christian Scripture as the authoritative source of spiritual information. Some were even able to cross the Protestant-Catholic gulf.

Not everyone approves of the above approach. Some churches with a more fundamentalist perspective choose not to be involved in such ministry because it involves the spectrum of Protestant noted above and some Catholics. They have not criticized the message the ministry promoted: that the God revealed in the Bible is God and salvation comes only through Jesus Christ, and the Bible is the reliable guide to spiritual truth; but they let some of their other doctrines keep them from the spiritual unity of such ministry. It is hard for me to reconcile such behavior by followers of Jesus with Jesus' prayer in John 17 and the example of the early church.

It is my prayer and my hope that every Christian who is exposed to the ideas of Classic Christian Realism will understand that God expects him or her to be responsive to the prayer of Jesus in John 17 AND then I hope and pray that person will have the wisdom to follow the example that the early church provides for us so that God may bless us and work powerfully though us to achieve His purposes.

Appendix A.

COMPARISON OF CONTEMPORARY CHRISTENDOM WITH THE EARLY CHURCH

T HE EARLY CHURCH had characteristics that contemporary Christianity would do well to emulate. If Christianity today adopted a behavior of the early church that facilitated spiritual unity, it might facilitate God working more powerfully through Christianity today than He did in the past century.

For this book the "early church" is the church during its first two centuries. Thus the "early church" covers church history from its beginning at the Day of Pentecost (sometime in the 30s) to about 240 A.D. During this period Christianity was generally opposed by local leaders, occasionally subject to widespread persecution, in competition with a host of established religions for the hearts and minds of people,[73] and beset with a variety of heresies within Christendom.[74]

Because it seems that God worked more powerfully through the early church than He has through the church in the past century, the behavior of the early church in some ways may be worth emulating. In support of this idea, this appendix compares the early church and Christendom of the past century to see if the premise that God worked more powerfully through the early church is valid.

It is important to pick a reasonable criterion for evaluating how powerfully God works in comparing the power of God's work through the early church with His work through contemporary Christendom during the past century. Both eras are long enough (a century or two) that a brief and unusual expression of God's power should not unduly bias the evaluation.

Since the Day of Pentecost, ten days after Jesus ascended into heaven, God has redeemed sinful men, women, and children through His power, granting them forgiveness for their sins and giving them eternal life.[75] That aspect of God's power has been demonstrated continuously since the church began. However, such is not something we humans can use to compare for assessing the demonstration of God's power in the church because we cannot see into the human heart to distinguish the true believer from the phony one. Think about this carefully. How many would be prone to say a person who preached in Jesus' name and who did amazing things in Jesus' name, even casting out evil spirits in the name of Jesus, was a great Christian? Many would call such a person a great follower of Jesus but Jesus described some like that as those He never knew (Matthew 7:21-23). The greatest theologians of the church over the centuries have been unable to say how to correctly identify the Elect on earth every time. Therefore this discussion which compares two eras of church history is not about that aspect of God's power, His forgiveness of human sin.

In the Old Testament, miraculous events (healings, dead people becoming alive again, dividing of the Red Sea or the Jordan River, etc.) do not occur with the same frequency throughout the millennium from Moses to the Babylonian Captivity nor equally throughout all of Judea and Israel. Hence it would be foolish to try to compare two eras of church history by looking at such things in the two eras.

Many ways to assess the spiritual vitality, health, etc. of the church in a geographic area or in an era of time have been suggested. Most suggestions pick a characteristic or two of the church as the basis for evaluation. For example, some would use the level of missionary support by churches as an indication of spirituality since that is related to bringing the gospel to the lost so they can be saved. That evaluation criterion would say that some of the smaller denominations with a missionary abroad for every hundred or two of church members are much more alive spiritually than a mainline denomination which might have only one missionary abroad for every 5-10,000 members. Of course, that particular evaluation criterion makes the Moravian Brethren of the 18th century stand head and shoulders above every other group and puts everyone else to shame.[76]

Some suggest that commitment of the followers of Jesus is a primary factor that causes God to work powerfully through the church; and note that there was opposition to Christianity from leaders in most locali-ties and sometimes Christians in the Roman Empire faced persecution Empire-wide. Estimates of the portion of believers martyred in the early church are sometimes as high as 10%, but it is more likely that the number killed was a smaller percentage.[77] Sometimes those considered martyred were only confined and tortured, or had their possession taken. This commitment of the followers of Jesus is asserted as the reason that God worked so powerfully in the early church by those that would make this a factor that caused God to work powerfully during that era.

Many have felt such to be the case. Tertullian (~155-240 A.D.), a theolo-gian of the early church who lived in Carthage, North Africa, wrote "The blood of martyrs is the seed of the church." Many others have repeated that sentiment; but it does not seem actually to be true. Based upon infor-mation from 221 nations and territories, when the current level of restric-tion on religion is plotted versus church growth, there does not seem to be such a correlation.[78] Some who make this claim seem to be unaware that probably more Christians were martyred in the 20th century than in the previous nineteen centuries combined.[79] Hence that perspective does not explain why God worked more powerfully in the early church than He has in contemporary Christendom.

The parameter used here to compare the power of God's work through two eras of church history (the early church and contemporary Christendom) is the growth in those claiming to be followers of Jesus Christ, i.e., the growth in Christendom measured by the percent of the population associ-ated with Christianity. This criterion avoids the problem of determining-which members of Christendom are born-again Christians (or whatever other way one might use to describe God's Elect on earth). Estimates pertinent to the criterion exist already; none needed to be generated for this book.

This parameter is not a perfect indicator of God's power. Some might profess to follow Christ for unspiritual reason. Many Jews did that in medieval Europe to save their lives or property. Some did it on the mis-sion field simply for material benefits associated with being a follower of Christ; "rice Christians" was coined to describe such folk. However, this parameter provides an indication of God's power in spreading the claims of Christ on people through the church. Hence that is the evalua-tion criterion that will be used here.

God in His sovereignty can choose to act powerfully or not to act powerfully whenever He chooses, with or without an obvious relationship to anything that Christians may be doing. However, generally God chooses to act in accord with His revelation of how He acts. Hence it is pertinent to ask if there is anything in the Scripture that might relate to when or why God may work powerfully through His church. There is; it is found in the prayer of Jesus in John 17. Jesus prayed that His followers (both the apostles and those who will believe through them) might be one so the world would believe that the Father sent Him. This suggests that unity among the followers of Jesus causes God to work powerfully to bring people to faith in Jesus.

A.1. Expansion of Contemporary Christendom in the Past Century

Contemporary Christendom has major advantages over the early church in logistics (e.g., transportation and movement of people and things) and communications (print, letters and mail, phone-radio-TV-internet, etc.) as well as far greater resources (people, funds, and facilities) for evangelism. Yet the portion of the world population within Christendom for the past century has been stagnant at about a third in spite of the vast resources and population of Christendom.[80] Hence the conclusion that God has not been working as powerfully through the church in our time as will be shown for His work through the early church; however, the following caveats apply to that conclusion.

In Europe and the Americas, especially the U.S., Christendom seems to be shrinking as the portion of the population identified as unreligious, agnostic, or atheist increases. Elsewhere in the world persecutions (some of which are basically genocides or ethnic cleansings) have reduced the number of Christians during the past century. Such persecutions include the Armenian massacre of Christians by the Turks, Egyptian persecution of Coptic Christians, communist killing of millions of Christians in Russia and China, and Islamic killing of Christians in Nigeria and Syria. Hence the portion of world population in Christendom has been stagnant for the past century, in part because 1-2% of the Christian population was martyred during that century. Many in American churches, including their ministers and others with formal theological training, have no idea of the magnitude of the slaughter of Christians in the twentieth century.[81]

There's another factor that also needs to be considered: the spurt in world population growth rate in the 20th century. Until about 1800 world population had grown slowly. Advances in medicine, sanitation improvements, more food available, etc. allowed the world population to increase nearly 50% in the 1800s; but in the 1900s (the twentieth century) world population quadrupled! Hence for Christendom to maintain a third of the world's population in Christendom, a great many people had to be attracted to Christianity since much of the world's population growth was in parts of the world which were not nominally Christian.

A.2. Expansion of the Early Church

The early church covers from the 30s to about 240 A.D. During this period, Christendom grew from a handful of Jewish followers of Jesus in the Roman Province of Syria (which includes Galilee, Samaria, and Judea)[82] to a religion of both Jew and Gentile from all social and ethnic groups (Jew and Gentile, rich and poor, slave and free, male and female, adult and child, etc.) that numbered about 10% of the population in the Roman Empire[83] plus followers of Jesus in Armenia,[84] the Parthian Empire, and parts of India. This happened within the constraints of logistic and communication limitations[85] in antiquity, in the presence of opposition to Christianity from local authorities, occasional widespread persecution, competing religions,[86] and heresies within Christendom.[87]

This remarkable growth (from a handful of people to a significant portion of the Roman Empire in two centuries) makes it appear that God worked more powerfully through the early church than He has done in the past century (since the Christendom portion of world population is been approximately constant). Why did God work so much more powerfully through the early church than He seems to be doing today?

Of course, it could be simply that God chose to do so in His sovereignty; but there may be more to it than that. While God chooses to do things based upon His decision about what is best for His purposes, it is also true that God generally works in accordance with His revelation of Himself. Jesus prayed for spiritual unity among His followers the night before He was arrested. He said that unity would show the world that the Father had sent Him.

Currently Christendom is splintered into hundreds, even thousands of groups (denominations, churches, sects, organizations, etc.),[88] many of which will not work together with some of the other groups for religious purposes (such as worship services, evangelism, discipleship, etc.) or to provide social help for the needy. That divisiveness may limit how God chooses to work through the church.

Sometimes divisions within Christendom are driven by beliefs (sometimes those beliefs are fundamental to the Christian faith, and other times they are more secondary). Sometimes the divisions are driven by organizational and political reasons (this especially has been true in national churches and in regard to control of religious material resources such as funds and property).[89] Sometimes the divisions are driven by personalities of the group's leader (this has especially been true in modern times because technology has enabled an individual to communicate with multitudes in ways that were not possible in the past).

Both the New Testament and the writings of Christendom during the early church show that motivations for such divisiveness existed then as it does now (this is dealt with explicitly by the Apostle Paul in 1 Corinthians 3 as he addressed divisions associated with various leaders; he pointed the Corinthians back to Christ and the importance of working together for Him.), but the early church kept a primary focus on the primary truths about the Triune Godhead and His plan of salvation through faith in Jesus, whose death and resurrection makes that salvation possible for sinful people.

The question here is how to demonstrate that primary focus of the early church. Contemporary material from and about the early church is very limited, and much of what survives is basically from quotation by later sources of what was written, said, or done by those earlier. Leaders in the early church addressed many topics, from the messages they communicated to those not yet followers of Jesus to details about how followers of Jesus should behave in communications to those who were within the church.

These difficulties led to the following approach. The early church struggled to summarize its basic beliefs so that such could be used as a check on what one who belonged to it should profess. This led to the idea that what was emphasized in the earliest such summaries of Christian belief would indicate the things considered of primary importance by the early church. Hence that is the approach used in this book to indicate what the early church focused upon and emphasized.

Unfortunately, no such summaries from the early church itself have survived; initial formulation of the earliest such summaries that survive to the current day come from about a century after the early church. It is reasonable to assume that what is emphasized in those extant early summaries were what was emphasized in the summaries that no longer exist and the extant early summaries provide a reasonable indication of what was emphasized by the early church. Those extant summaries are the Apostles' Creed and the Nicene Creed.

A way to check that this approach provides a reliable indication of what the early church emphasized is to examine the sermons and material presented to non-Christians in the Book of Acts. They too emphasize what is emphasized in these early creeds: the nature of God and His plan of salvation. Because the epistles of the New Testament are written to Christians, they focus mainly on other things (especially how Christians should live). The two exceptions are Romans and Hebrews, both of which were written to those that the writer did not know well (in contrast, writers and recipients of most epistles in the New Testament knew one another quite well).

The Apostles' Creed and the Nicene Creed are used to indicate the topics of primary emphasis in the early church (the nature of God and His plan of salvation); their particular expression of those topics suffer from something that often affects summaries of Christian belief. The creeds try to express belief in ways that are more comprehensive philosophically and logically than is actually said in Scripture. Such can go beyond what the Scripture actually says, and tie the basic concept presented to a particular form of expression. Sometimes groups of believers have divided over the way a particular concept is expressed when all involved can affirm the words used in the Scripture; such can create most unfortunate and unnecessary divisions within Christendom.

The two creeds used to indicate the focus of the early church emphasize the nature of God (Three Person-One God Being of the Scripture and the Divine-Human nature of the Son of God) and God's plan of salvation for people by its reference to the Son of God Who died and rose again to make human salvation possible. Unfortunately, many today seem to put so much emphasis on important but secondary things that capability to work with others to serve Christ with spiritual unity gets restricted.

This has been illustrated repeatedly by the way some fundamentalist and evangelical churches refuse to participate in broad Christian endeavors (such as a city-wide evangelistic campaign, a ministry serving prisoners in the local jail, etc.) because some involved in the group do not profess their view of Biblical inerrancy (or another important doctrine that group emphasizes) even though all involved in the endeavor profess faith in the Triune Godhead and His salvation through faith in Jesus.

Individual writers in the early church addressed many aspects of Christian belief and practice, but they all emphasized what was in those creeds. This basically provided the spiritual unity among congregations throughout Christendom which God seems to have used to convince people that the Father had sent Jesus for their salvation. Those whom the early church largely rejected, such as indicated by those promoting the heresies mentioned in a footnote earlier, did not hold to the truths about the nature of God and His plan of salvation expressed in the two creeds.

In addition to its focus on the primary truths of Christianity (and the associated spiritual unity which that permitted), commitment of Christians in the early church to Christ was generally greater than that by many within Christendom today. The social and political benefits of belonging to a favored religious group did not come to Christians in the early church since identification as a follower of Jesus often brought opposition and persecution; estimates suggest that perhaps 10% of Christians in the Early Church experienced confinement, material loss, or martyrdom because of their faith. Even though there were many Christian martyrs during the twentieth century, it appears that the rate of such was greater in the early church than it was in the past century.[90] The commitment of followers of Christ in areas where Christianity is not held in high regard (now or in the early church) contrasts dramatically with the lackadaisical commitment to Christ manifested by many in Europe and the U.S. who do not even participate regularly in worship services of the church to which they belong.

CCR contends that God's powerful work in the early church was facilitated by the spiritual unity of believers and their serious commitment to Christ; then CCR contends that its perspective will facilitate spiritual unity within the contemporary church and clarify the differences between Christianity's approach to reality from that of materialists (which should help followers of Jesus to be more serious about their commitment to Christ). It is believed that such might allow or cause God to act more powerfully through the church than He has in the past century or so. It is recognized that there are many followers of Christ who live in societies that are hostile to Christianity (such as communist or Muslim nations) and growth in the church there from God's powerful work is probably offset by Christendom's losses in Europe and the Americas.

The contentions just stated cannot be proven, or perhaps not even fully justified by information currently available. In part, that is fundamental for two reasons. First, we cannot always tell when God acts simply in accordance with His revelation of His patterns of behavior or when He has chosen to do (or not do) something for other reasons. Any reading of the historical books of the Old Testament makes that very clear. Second, it is also true that we cannot tell who the Elect on earth are with high accuracy. Two comments from the Gospels illustrate the problem. Jesus describes some in Matthew 7:21-23 that most Christians would think are great disciples of Jesus: they preach in His name, do mighty works (miracles) in His name, and even cast out demons in His name. However, Jesus totally rejects them and says He "never knew them." In Mark 12:41-44 Jesus commends the small offering of a widow as greater than that by everyone else. Human limited perception of things and our corrupted evaluation system do not always enable our judgment to be that of Jesus. Theologians over the centuries have struggled with how to identify God's Elect here on earth (it will be easy to identify them in heaven: they will be the people there). No one has figured out how to identify the Elect here on earth with complete accuracy.[91]

Sometimes one finds confirmation of a point in a most unexpected place. That happened in regard to what this book contends was the basis for spiritual unity in the early church: their commitment to the basic beliefs of Christianity ("the faith" in the comment below) and not allowing secondary things to interfere with that. That particular confirmation was found in the following words about Christianity in ancient Mesopotamia, an area that covers modern Iran, Syria, bits of Turkey, and more. There were significant numbers of Christians in that area during the first seven centuries of church history. "Until the end of the third century, the unity which existed among the different Churches was guaranteed not by ecclesiastical structure but by the unity of the faith." This quote is from page 8 of *The Church in Iraq* (publish in 2017 by Fernando Cardinal Filoni, who has been head of missionary endeavors for the Roman Catholic Church since 2011) as he described the beginnings of Christianity in that geographic area.[92] The quote covers all of what this book calls the "early church" plus several decades. The comment is particular significant since Filoni focuses on ecclesiastical structure mainly in his discussion of two millennia of church history in that area.

A.3. Comments about Contemporary Christianity and the Early Church

There are a number of similarities between Christendom of the twentieth century and the early church. Both experienced significant persecution. A far greater number were martyred because they were Christians in the twentieth century than in the two centuries of the early church; but that was because of the far greater population. The percent of followers of Jesus martyred during the early church was probably several times greater than the percentage of Christians martyred in the twentieth century.

Also similar is a belief in one God and that Jesus is the Savior. Of course, there are many variations in what exactly is and was believed by those within Christendom in each of those times. The measure being used in comparison of the two eras (the percentage of the population associated with Christianity) makes no effort to distinguish "true believers" (the "Elect") from others within the church or associated with Christianity; it is unknown how much that impacts the reliability of the measure as a surrogate indication of the level of power in God's working in the church during the eras but CCR assumes that it does not invalidate the measure's use for its intended purpose.

Both eras faced competing ideologies. In the early church, the competing ideologies were mainly the claims of ethnic loyalties and other religions practiced in the locality. In the twentieth century, competing ideologies came from Islam and indigenous religions in Africa and Asia, communism, and secular humanism.

In both eras, the penetration of Christianity in the population varied significantly by location. For example, some peoples of the world (such as in the Americas, islands in the Pacific such as Hawaii or Japan, regions of Asia far from the Roman Empire) were not exposed to Christianity at all during the early church. In the twentieth century, there was a much lower percentage of the population associated with Christianity in Moslem countries and in Asia than in the U.S. or Europe.

In addition to the similarities of the two eras, there were a number of differences. During the early church, world population changed very little; but during the 20th century, it quadrupled. During the early church, travel and communication were slow and expensive. During the twentieth century, travel was fast and communication (mail, phone, radio, TV, and internet) ubiquitous and relatively cheap. During the early church, life expectancy was low (less than 40, greatly influenced by the high rate of death for infants and young children); during the twentieth century life expectancy was more than double the life expectancy of the early church era.

There also are many areas where comparison of Christendom in the 20th century with the early church is impossible because of lack of reliable information about the early church. For example, it is unclear what kind of administrative relationships existed among different congregations, religious leaders, religious schools, etc. During the early church group meetings were held in private homes or public areas; this is illustrated in the New Testament in Acts when the followers of Jesus met in Jerusalem and in references in the epistles to congregations meeting in individual homes. Buildings specifically for Christian activities only began to appear toward the end of the early church. The Dura-Europos church (also known as the Dura-Europos house church) is the earliest identified Christian house church.[93]

Appendix B.

SPIRITUAL UNITY

A PRIMARY OBJECTIVE OF this book is to promote spiritual unity among the followers of Jesus Christ in response to Jesus' prayer in John 17. It is important that what is meant by such spiritual unity be clearly explicated because there are many connotations associated with unity. This appendix provides that explication.

For some, unity is the lack of active conflict among groups. This is perhaps the lowest connotation for unity and is the kind of unity expected from those who emphasize tolerance in America's growing religious plurality. The unity Jesus seeks for His followers is more than lack of active conflict among groups.

For some, unity merely reflects common purpose. This kind of unity is found among allies in a war, even though the allies may have radically different political systems and aspirations beyond defeat of their common enemy. Others talk about unity among diverse people and groups in an endeavor such as "save the children" or "save the whales." The unity Jesus seeks for His followers is more than unity derived from sharing a common purpose.

For some, unity comes from a shared mood. Such unity may be manifested at a rock concert, by partisans at a football game as the crowd chants and sways in unison, or in an emotionally expressive religious service. The unity Jesus seeks for His followers is more than unity derived from a shared mood.

For others, unity comes from a shared ideology. In Howard County, Maryland (where the author of this book lives), the public library urges people to "choose civility" which is intended to promote unity in civil behavior by those in the community. Some find unity in sharing a political ideology, a cultural identity, or a particular religion. The unity Jesus seeks for His followers is more than unity derived from a shared ideology.

The spiritual unity that Jesus seeks for His followers has aspects of all the kinds of unity mentioned (lack of conflict, shared purpose, shared mood, and shared ideology), but the unity Jesus seeks for His followers is more than all of these approaches to unity combined.

B.1. The Spiritual Unity Jesus Seeks for His Followers

Jesus did not pray that all people would have spiritual unity. The Scripture is clear that Jesus came so that salvation would be possible for anyone. Jesus declared that in His discussion with Nicodemus. "For God so loved the world, that He gave His only Son, that whoever believes in Him should not perish but have eternal life." (John 3:16 ESV) However, Jesus' prayer in John 17 is not for the world (all people). Instead He prayed for His followers: the ones who were with Him that night and those who would believe that He was sent from the Father by what those who were with Him said. Jesus said, [20] "I do not ask for these only, but also for those who will believe in me through their word, [21] that they may all be one, just as you, Father, are in me, and I in you, that they also may be in us, so that the world may believe that you have sent me." (John 17:20-21 ESV) Exactly who Jesus means in these words is clear from what He says earlier in His prayer: "[12] While I was with them, I kept them in your name, which you have given me. I have guarded them, and not one of them has been lost except the son of destruction, that the Scripture might be fulfilled." (John 17:12 ESV) He is referring to the Twelve minus Judas.[94] Tradition says only one of these eleven men died a natural death (John); the others were martyred (as tradition says was also the fate of Matthias, the one who replaced Judas).

In simple terms, the only ones that Jesus prayed would have spiritual unity are His followers. This excludes all who reject Jesus: Jews that do not consider Him to be the Messiah, Moslems who accept Jesus as a prophet but deny He is the divine Savior, atheists who deny existence of God, and materialists who deny His involvement in the world at this time, and all who ignore Jesus (the unevangelized through their ignorance of Him, and those who do not commit themselves to Him for salvation, including those in "Christian" churches who were baptized as infants but never as a mature person profess faith in Jesus). Unfortunately there are fuzzy thinkers around who do not pay close attention to what Jesus actually says and instead substitute muddle-headed ideas about unity among all people. Some will find this candor offensive; an apology is offered for offending them, but there is no apology for the truth of what is said.

The spiritual unity that Jesus prayed for is possible because of spiritual reality revealed in Christian Scripture. That spiritual reality is what Christ did in redeeming people. He not only bridged the gulf between a holy God and sinful people, He removed all barriers between people racially, gender-wise, and socially. He did this because His followers are in Him and He is in them. Thus, for the followers of Jesus, the ones who have been born-again and put into His body, the church universal, there are no racial distinctions (Jew or Gentile), no sexual distinctions (male or female), and no social distinctions (free or slave, rich or poor, wise or otherwise, etc.). The reader is urged to consider all that the Scripture says about the saved being in Christ.

The early church provides an imperfect example of such spiritual unity. This book contends that the early church's example of spiritual unity came from proper priority that focused on spreading the gospel by emphasizing the primary truths (who God is and His plan of salvation) without permitting secondary things (not even important doctrines such as the doctrines about baptism, church organization, and Scriptural inspiration) to impede that emphasis of the primary truths. That example is "imperfect" because even in the early church they did not always do things right. Such imperfection is illustrated by the Apostle Paul.

Acts 13 indicates that Barnabas and Saul were chosen by the Holy Spirit to go as missionaries to a Gentile land (Cyprus); John Mark accompanied them. During the early part of their mission to Cyprus, Acts switches from calling Saul (his Jewish name) to calling him by his Roman name (Paul), and that is basically how he is referenced (as Paul) for the rest of Acts and in epistles of the New Testament since from that point on in Paul's life he is primarily involved in ministry to Gentiles in the Roman Empire. At some point, Paul (now listed first in the missionary team) and his companions leave Cyprus and go to what is modern Turkey; John Mark leaves them and returns to Jerusalem. No explanation for any of these things is given in Acts or mentioned by other contemporary writers.

Eventually Paul's missionary team returns to Antioch from which they had been sent to Cyprus and reports about their ministry to Gentiles. Dissention about what was necessary for salvation (especially for salvation of Gentiles) led to the Council of Jerusalem (Acts 15), where it was settled that Gentile believers did not have to become Jewish converts in order to be saved by Jesus. Some time after that, Paul wants to return to every city where the missionary team had ministered. When John Mark wants to go with them to where they began (Cyprus), Paul objected (Acts 15:36-41). This created disunity; but God even used that to His glory. Barnabas and John Mark go to Cyprus (where the missionary team had gone first), and Paul and Silas go to central Turkey where the missionary team had gone from Cyprus.

The Scripture simply says what happened, but does not explain why these things happened. It is possible that Paul was miffed at John Mark for not going along with Paul and the others when the team left Cyprus for central Turkey (although John Mark had performed the assignment he committed to), and the disunity was a result of Paul's attitude. Likewise it is possible Paul was justified in rejecting John Mark as an unreliable worker, and disunity came when Barnabas (John Mark's kinsman) demanded that John Mark be part of the missionary team. Whether one of these possibilities or something else was cause for the disunity, a split in the missionary endeavor occurred. Later comments about John Mark by Paul suggest the disunity over him went away. Some think there was more than one person referenced by the name Mark in the New Testament, but most think all the Mark references in Acts and the epistles refer to the same person, the one that tradition says was an associate of Peter and wrote the Gospel of Mark.

The spiritual unity that Jesus seeks for His followers is important because it causes the world to believe that Jesus was sent by the Father. That is central to what Jesus told His followers to do in His last words to them according to the Scripture: "you will be my witnesses in Jerusalem and in all Judea and Samaria, and to the end of the earth." (Acts 1:8 ESV) The central message of Christians to the world is that the Father sent Jesus to be the Savior, with explanation for how to accept Him as Savior. This gives spiritual unity among the followers of Jesus special importance.

The spiritual unity that Jesus seeks for His followers is the spiritual unity that this book encourages. It is a unity among followers of Jesus (those whom He has saved and who are in Him) that enables them to cooperate with other followers of Jesus in worship, evangelism, discipleship, and helping the needy. Such unity is made possible by what happened to the people when Christ saved them. They were put into Christ and the Holy Spirit began to dwell within them. This reality is what allows God to see the righteousness of Christ for the saved, and all of them being in Christ is the reality that makes the spiritual unity Jesus prayed for possible.

Such spiritual unity does not require that everyone be in the same religious organization or that there be formal arrangements among religious organizations, although spiritual unity may be manifested within such situations. Expression of spiritual unity of an individual follower of Jesus with other followers of Jesus should not be impeded by actions of religious organizations. All who acknowledge and worship the Father-Son-Holy Spirit God revealed in the Scripture and accept His plan of salvation through faith in Jesus Christ should manifest spiritual unity because they have the spiritual unity of being in Christ. Impediments imposed by religious organization that prevent or limit how such followers of Jesus can worship together, evangelize and disciple others, and help the needy are contrary to Jesus' prayer for spiritual unity among His followers.

Those manifesting spiritual unity are not always involved with everyone else in every spiritual endeavor. This is illustrated by the church at Antioch in the New Testament, the place where followers of Jesus were first called Christians (Acts 11:26). All of the Christians in Antioch were involved in sending help to needy Christians in Jerusalem, but not all of them went with Barnabas and Saul to deliver that help to Jerusalem (Acts 11:27-30). Likewise, a number of leaders of the church at Antioch were led to set Barnabas and Soul off on their first missionary journey, but they did not go with them. Thus, a Christian who manifests spiritual unity may be led by God to do other things than participate in a particular spiritual activity (whether worship, evangelism, discipleship, or helping the needy) that others are doing (whether or not those others are part of or outside the person's religious organization).

B.2. Plain Talk about Spiritual Unity

The spiritual unity that Jesus prayed His followers would have is based upon that fact that born-again Christians are in Christ. That spiritual unity is manifested by the love a Christian shows for other followers of Jesus, by openness to worship and cooperation with anyone sharing belief in the Triune God revealed in the Scripture and His plan of salvation in Christian ministry, and by cooperating with such people in helping the needy. This provides a functional description of the spiritual unity this book promotes.

Such spiritual unity often is impeded by human pride, institutions, and failures (especially failure by Christians to love other followers of Jesus). For example, human pride may have had a role in Paul's snit over John Mark described in Acts 15. Human pride is the cause of partiality (such as based upon social status) that James 2 warns against; such pride also causes disunity spiritually.

Human institutions can impede spiritual unity. This may be one reason that the New Testament provides such limited guidance about administrative organization for Christian society, whether in its religious or political aspects. Church administrative structures historically have often been a major hindrance to spiritual unity: some call themselves the only "true church" and set walls around themselves and declare all outside them as unsaved, outside the body of Christ. Some relatively small religious groups do this; and so have large churches. Some of the churches doing that began in antiquity and others began in modern times. History demonstrates that such a claim has to be invalid. No religious group in the first several centuries of Christianity had administrative or organizational contact with all segments of Christendom (every segment of which claimed connection to foundation by one or more of the apostles). Today, the largest Christian group (the 24 autonomous *sui iuris* particular Catholic churches: the Latin Catholic Church and the 23 Eastern Catholic Churches which comprise the Catholic Church[95]) contain only about half of the population of Christendom; fewer than 20% of Catholics claim to be born-again Christians[96], whereas most members of a number of other churches in Christendom claim to be born-again.

Human institutions can be an impediment to the spiritual unity Jesus prayed for when the institution establishes walls and excludes those who profess similar (or identical belief) in the Triune Godhead and His plan of salvation as professed by that institution. Unfortunately such is done by many groups within Christendom today.

Human failures also can impede spiritual unity when followers of Jesus are unwilling to join others in worship, evangelism, discipleship, or help for the needy because of racial, ethnic, political, or social differences. Human failures also can impede spiritual unity when emphasis on secondary doctrines (whether based in Scripture or just church traditions) interferes with worship, evangelism, discipleship, or helping the needy with others who share beliefs about who God is and His plan of salvation. Such human failures impede spiritual unity and consequently cause

God to work less powerfully through the church than He might have done otherwise.

This book places the onus for spiritual unity on the individual follower of Jesus, whether or not the religious organization (church or group) in which the individual participates promotes the kind of spiritual unity emphasized in this book. It would be great if every Christian organization promoted the spiritual unity advocated by this book, but that seems unlikely to happen. It is important for every Christian to realize that he or she is accountable to God, and each will have to account to God for the way he or she responds to (or doesn't respond to) the prayer of Jesus for spiritual unity among His followers.

B.3. Examples of Spiritual Unity (and Disunity) in Contemporary Christianity

During four decades plus of involvement in Christian ministry to inmates, inmate families and former inmates, correctional institutional staff, and ministry volunteers, the author of this book saw a number of instances of spiritual unity among followers of Christ that is similar to that demonstrated by the early church. A few examples of such are described here, without identifying the specific situations in which they occurred. These examples are the sort that individual followers of Jesus can relate to. They are the kinds of things individual believers can do.

These examples of spiritual unity are drawn from ministries under the auspices of non-government organizations (in contrast to ministries under the auspices of government-employed chaplains).[97] The examples of impediments to spiritual unity also relate to ministries under the auspices of non-government organizations.

These simple examples demonstrate that spiritual unity is possible even for very diverse elements of Christendom if proper priorities are maintained by those involved; the examples also show that allowing secondary things to assume inappropriate importance can impede spiritual unity, thwarting the prayer of Jesus in John 17.

B.3.1. Example 1 of Spiritual Unity Behind Bars

Typically worship services at the correctional institution were handled by several different church groups, each of which would lead a worship service once a month or once a quarter (the church leading the worship service would provide musicians and a song leader, perhaps a choir or musical group such as a trio to perform a special number, and speakers to deliver the sermon, give testimonies, read Scripture, etc.). When there were gaps in the schedule because a church had dropped out or could not make its normal assignment, a team of volunteers from different churches would provide leadership for the worship service. The members of that team came from a variety of churches (typically the team for a particular service would come from 4-5 different churches; the collection of churches that might be represented by at least one person on one team during the year included AME, Assembly of God, Baptist, Church of God, community, Episcopal, independent, Lutheran, Methodist, and Presbyterian churches. The people in the team shared a commitment to the God of the Christian Scripture, a belief in salvation by faith in Jesus, and a love for other Christians. This (their spiritual unity) is why they could minister together in the worship service in spite of many differences in their beliefs about baptism, communion, church organization and structure, etc.

B. 3. 2. Example 2 of Spiritual Unity Behind Bar

A particular ministry had a program of discipleship training that used a volunteer to meet with the same inmate week after week providing both structured training and relationship building by the volunteer and inmate praying together, sharing insights and concerns, etc. The structured training involved the *Survival Kit for New Christians* and similar material. Typically the volunteers in this ministry came from evangelical Protestant churches. The chaplain noticed that inmates who attended Catholic services seem to feel uncomfortable in the one-on-one discipleship sessions with evangelical Protestant volunteers (such volunteers often had little appreciation of the mindset that many Catholic inmates possessed). So the chaplain approached folks involved in Catholic services at the institution to see if any would be willing to get involved with the discipleship training program and work in it with Catholic inmates using the same materials and processes as already used in the program. Some of those involved in Catholic services were willing and after getting the same training as the Protestant volunteers, those Catholic volunteers began to minister in discipleship training focused on Catholic inmates. This is another example of the kind of spiritual unity demonstrated by the early church; it was very helpful to inmates.

B. 3. 3. Example 3 of Spiritual Unity in Correctional Ministry

This example comes from the community and has two components. One component involves financial support of a ministry inside a correctional institution. Over a period of years, financial contributions for this ministry (which most would classify as a typical ministry of evangelical Christianity) has come from a variety of Protestant churches as well as from individuals and a few businesses; in additional it has also received financial support from a few Catholic churches. That is an indication of spiritual unity.

Sometimes things are done in the community for a correctional ministry as well as behind bars in an institution. Many correctional ministries emphasize inmate study of Christian Scripture. Some provide inmates with Bible correspondence courses. Completed inmate lessons from such courses are often graded by volunteers in the community. The collection of people grading such lessons from inmates at a particular correctional facility came from a wide variety of Protestant churches and from some Catholic churches. They all use the same grading keys to score inmate lessons, and they write encouraging comments on the lessons. This too illustrates spiritual unity when Christians from diverse churches work together to bring inmates to Christ and to encourage their spiritual growth. This is the second component of Example 3.

B. 3. 4. Example 1 of Impediments to Ministry and to Spiritual Unity

Ministry in a local jail had a policy of focusing on salvation by faith in Jesus and the Bible as a guide for proper belief and living. All volunteers in this ministry agreed to leave their denominational distinctives outside the jail and comply with all jail regulations.

Sometimes the ministry had to dismiss volunteers for failing to abide by those guidelines. One man had to be dismissed for extending his visits with inmates far beyond the scheduled time; he just had so much to share as they studied the Bible. Of course, this upset the schedule correctional officers expected and interfered with other jail operations. The man persisted in that behavior though chided for it several times; each time he apologized and promised to follow the rules, but he didn't. So he had to be fired as a volunteer.

Another volunteer failed to keep his church's beliefs about spiritual signs outside the jail, and kept telling inmates that unless they manifested certain spiritual signs they were not first-class Christians and might not even be saved. That volunteer had to be fired also.

These situations show how failure to comply with established ministry policies and institutional rules can impede both a ministry and spiritual unity. Removal from the ministry team of those failing to comply was necessary to prevent disruption of the ministry.

B. 3. 5. Example 2 of an Impediment to Spiritual Unity

A church in the community refused to participate in a correctional ministry. That church's doctrine about religious associations kept it from being part of the ministry because some of the ministry's volunteers belonged to particular kinds of churches even though the pastor of the church refusing to participate in the ministry said he saw no problem in the ministry's statement of belief or in the materials that the ministry distributed to inmates. However, elevation of some of the church's doctrine kept that church from being responsive to the prayer of Jesus in John 17.

Concern about the truth revealed by the Scripture is important. Sound doctrine is important. Keeping priorities proper spiritually is also important. This is a point that Jesus addresses specifically at times in His criticism of some religious practices for letting lesser important things impede the more important (e.g., Matthew23:23; Mark 2:23-28).

Appendix C.

SENSUS PLENIOR AND SIMILAR METHODS OF INTERPRETATION

T HE PRIMARY MEANING of a Scriptural passage is determined by taking what the text says in its normal meaning (i.e., its normal literal significance with appropriate adaptation for passages which employ figurative language) with due attention to the context of the passage. However, sometimes there is also a deeper or additional meaning for a passage of Scripture. The reality and appropriateness of such additional meaning to some Scriptural passages is illustrated by some of the interpretations of Old Testament passages found in the New Testament.

Because the writers of the New Testament wrote under inspiration of the Holy Spirit, their interpretations of the Old Testament are correct. It is generally believed that there are passages in the Scripture with meaning beyond the normal (literal) meaning of what is said in addition to those passages so identified by New Testament writers. A variety of methods of interpretation (such as typological interpretation) have been employed to bring forth such addition (or deeper) meanings for Scriptural passages.

"Sensus plenior" (Latin for "fuller sense" or "fuller meaning") is used in Biblical interpretation to describe the supposed deeper meaning intended by God but perhaps not intended by the human author. It is thought that Andre Fernandez coined the term in 1927, but it was popularized by Roman Catholic theologian Raymond E. Brown in publication of his doctoral dissertation on the subject in the 1950s. Brown defines *sensus plenior* as "That additional, deeper meaning, intended by God but not clearly intended by the human author, which is seen to exist in the words of a biblical text (or group of texts, or even a whole book) when they are studied in the light of further revelation or development in the understanding of revelation."[98]

There are a number of instances of *sensus plenior* in Scripture which the Scripture itself identifies as fuller significance in an earlier passage of Scripture is explained by a later passage of Scripture. Because of the Holy Spirit's guidance for those whom God chose to produce the Scripture, such interpretation of the fuller sense of those passages is correct and can be accepted as true as we accept all Scripture is truth from God. And that is where the problem arises with *sensus plenior* as it does with all approaches seeking additional or fuller significance for Scriptural passages. How can anyone other than one God has chosen to produce the Scripture be sure an interpretation of the fuller sense of a Scripture passage is correct, and not just the imagination of the interpreter?[99] There is a major divide between the way many Protestants approach this subject and the way Catholics approach it; the divide exists because of their very different views regarding the role of church tradition.[100]

Potential for abuse of the *sensus plenior* concept is obvious. Some Protestants say that *sensus plenior* causes or contributes to Catholic Mariology; however that does not seem to be the case. Most Catholic doctrine about Mary comes from church tradition (sometimes elements of that doctrine have been reinforced or confirmed by *sensus plenior* interpretations in the past half century but *sensus plenior* is not its primary source).[101] Honesty and candor demands that *sensus plenior* and other approaches that seek additional or fuller significance from Biblical passages be considered in Biblical interpretation since reality shows such in Scripture by the inspired writers of New Testament Scripture. It has to be considered in proper Biblical interpretation. Addressing the hermeneutical challenge of *sensus plenior* is beyond the scope of this book; however, that such is a critical aspect of proper Biblical interpretation.[102]

Since several Protestant oriented discussions of *sensus plenior* have been references in footnotes and since the term *sensus plenior* and development of it initially in the twentieth century started in Catholic circles, it is appropriate to identify a contemporary perspective on *sensus plenior* within Catholicism. Such is available from Pauline A. Viviano, "The Senses of Scripture," *National Bible Week 2015* (available at http://www.usccb.org/bible/national-bible-week/upload/viviano-senses-scripture.pdf accessed September 2017).[103]

Appendix D.

IMPACT ON THE CHURCH OF SOCIAL PRIVILEGE AND POLITICAL ACCEPTANCE

HISTORY HAS SHOWN how social advantage and political acceptance has corrupted the church repeatedly. For example, Ryrie's 500 years of Protestant history (*Protestants*, Viking 2017) show repeated emphasis on church self-interest and privileges when dealing with adverse political environments such as European religious wars, Hitler's Germany, slavery era America, apartheid in South Africa, etc.; that focus often allowed other issues to be largely ignored, even very significant ones. There are horrible examples of evil behaviors by the church when it used political influence to banish, persecute, and kill those who disagreed with it; unfortunately such evil behaviors are not confined to one or a few varieties of groups within Christendom. Examples such as the centuries in which the inquisition functioned, the several centuries of witch-trials, and persecution of Anabaptists in Europe by both Protestants and Catholics are well-known. Even in its mildest forms, such as the "blue laws" in America,[104] exercise of political (legal) power by the church to force people to comply with its standards of behavior interferes with the Christian's primary mandate from Jesus to make disciples of all people. Christian discipleship must always be based upon a voluntary commitment to Jesus; not based upon physical or other compulsion (or inducement) to do something.

Society is always challenged by the basis it uses to set its standards of behavior. For many centuries, a number of standards have claimed some kind of basis in Christianity (in some cases those claims were even true). For example, some laws (such as those against theft, murder, and falsehood in court) have a solid basis in Scripture; and some of those laws also have a basis in other systems of ethics too. Many Christians are very concerned when our laws clearly contradict Biblical guidance; such as laws making homosexual activities generally acceptable legally. The early church provides one example of a way to act in such circumstances; Christians in the early church simply refused to worship idols or the emperor, and suffered for so doing but presented a witness to God's truth about such that put seeds in the minds and hearts of people that led to the salvation of some. The Christians behaving that way in the early church made no effort to gain control of the government and make laws according to what they thought was best. Some might choose that path today; and others might think it better to take a different approach.

One point is clear and undisputed: Christians should proclaim the truth revealed in God's Word. Not clear is what action is appropriate for Christians to take in shaping the laws where they live when circumstances (such as being in a democratic society) gives them opportunity to impact such laws. The author of this book is neither wise enough nor clever enough to provide general guidance about that complex issue.

In the past, some Christians have tolerated the evils of their society without rocking the boat. This seems to be what the Apostle Paul suggests in some of his epistles. Romans 13:1-7 is the passage most often cited in support of this approach: "[1] Let every person be subject to the governing authorities. For there is no authority except from God, and those that exist have been instituted by God. [2] Therefore whoever resists the authorities resists what God has appointed, and those who resist will incur judgment. [3] For rulers are not a terror to good conduct, but to bad. Would you have no fear of the one who is in authority? Then do what is good, and you will receive his approval, [4] for he is God's servant for your good. But if you do wrong, be afraid, for he does not bear the sword in vain. For he is the servant of God, an avenger who carries out God's wrath on the wrongdoer. [5] Therefore one must be in subjection, not only to avoid God's wrath but also for the sake of conscience. [6] For because of this you also pay taxes, for the authorities are ministers of God, attending to this very thing. [7] Pay to all what is owed to them: taxes to whom taxes are owed, revenue to whom revenue is owed, respect to whom respect is owed, honor to whom honor is owed." (ESV)

When Paul wrote Romans (probably from Corinth during his third missionary journey), in addition to local persecution of Christians, sometime previously Emperor Claudius had expelled Jews from Rome. That may have included Christians as a Jewish sect because of controversy over Christ, or so comments by the Roman historian Suetonius suggest. Nero was beginning his vicious reign. This is the context for the verses quoted above.

Christians in Hitler's Germany struggled with this kind of a situation in the 1930s and 1940s. The complex history of the decade-plus from Hitler's rise to leadership of Germany to the end of World War II illustrates the different ways that Christians wrestled with the situation and consequences for many of them.

Other Christians have tried to thwart some evils by defying the government and breaking the law to help those being oppressed. This is what some did who helped former slaves fleeing on the "underground railroad" before the American Civil War, and what some did in Hitler's domain as they helped Jews avoid concentration camps. Some deliberately break laws to get God's Word to people located where they cannot access Christian Scripture legally, such as done by Andrew van der Bijl (better known as Brother Andrew), a Christian missionary noted for his exploits smuggling Bibles to communist countries in the height of the Cold War, a feat that earned him the nickname "God's smuggler."

Some Christians have acted within the government to change what was being done. William Wilberforce is an example of such; his conversion to evangelical Christianity is recognized as a major factor in his successful efforts to end English involvement in the slave trade in the early years of the nineteenth century. God probably does not plan for all Christians to take the same approach in dealing with the ethical and moral issues of their time and situation; unfortunately, many Christians think everyone must accept the way that they see things in this area and adopt their approach or be condemned by them as doing wrong.

CCR's perspective is that it is dangerous for Christians as a community (i.e., the church or other religious organization) to be too closely associated with government organizationally because such is likely to compromise the clarity and vigor with which Christians can proclaim the truth of God. Such compromise in its message is probably the least of potential corruption from social privilege and political acceptance the church (or other Christian organization) would experience. All varieties of governments are prone to evil behavior at times, as shown repeatedly by history.

A church (or other Christian group) in bed with the government is likely to become involved in such evil behavior.

Consider the following. Christian chaplains in the military are expected to pray for the success of military endeavors, at the individual soldier, sailor, or air person level as well as for operations as a whole. The American military at times has engaged in activities that at least in hindsight were not just or proper. What about the chaplains' prayers in those situations? What would happen had a chaplain refused to pray for or encourage success in an operation? This shows how connection between church and state can corrupt the church even in what are normally considered appropriate kinds of activities.

The period chosen for the Early Church in this book was restricted to the first two centuries of church history because that avoided most of the potential for corruption from social privilege and political acceptance that Christianity experienced later. That allowed use of the Early Church as an example for dealing with the issue of spiritual unity before the pressures of cultural and political perspectives became as great as they are later in church history. This made the way the Early Church maintained its spiritual unity much clearer. That makes it easier for contemporary Christendom to emulate the Early Church in that regard.

A final comment about the potential dangers of social and political prominence for the church. The kind of situation described here appears repeatedly in church history. At times church leaders would behave like rascals to get their way and/or to elevate their positions within Christendom. This was illustrated in the 431 A.D. Council at Ephesus when Nestorius was condemned. Although Nestorius repeated proclaimed he believed that Jesus was truly God and truly man (which is consistent with what the Scripture actually says), because he did not accept the particular way that some in the church described the nature of the Son of God, the opponents of Nestorius forced the Council to act before representatives from churches in the East (which included churches in the Roman Province of Syria that contained Antioch, a center for Christianity since the days of the apostles) arrived so that the Council could condemn Nestorius and have him removed from the top spot in Constantinople (that allowed one of them to replace him). It was expected that those from the East would support Nestorius in this situation; which is why the Council acted before they arrived. This behavior of the 431 A.D. Council of Ephesus played a major role in split of Orthodox churches from Western Christendom of the Roman Catholic Church. It is depressing to realize how many major decisions within church history were made in such disgraceful ways. It helps one to always emphasis looking directly to the Scripture for God's truth, and makes one very cautious about the reliability of church tradition as a valid spiritual guide. Too much of it reflect motivations that are not good.

Christians are adapt at ignoring clear and explicit teachings of Jesus. In the Sermon on the Mount Jesus warns His disciples of the dangers of failing to show respect for others. He extends the prohibition against murder from the Mosaic Law to include anger, insults, and calling one a fool (Matthew 5:21-22). Even the most casual reading of church history shows the great disregard for these words from Jesus in what Christian leaders say about those who disagree with them. Those with dispensational inclinations may claim these words of Jesus apply to the Kingdom Age and are not applicable in the current Church Age; those with liberal tendencies may water down the consequences of behaving that way or explain things in some way that makes the words inapplicable to most people; and the rest of us are just likely to ignore what Jesus said. However, we should always take Jesus seriously.

This author hopes that what is said about those whose views differ from what was said in this book was done with appropriate respect for their right to their views and with appropriate respect for them as individuals; in addition, the author hopes views of others were not distorted. If any were, he apologizes and asks for information so he can correct his future comments.

LIMITED INDEX

BASIC WORKS

T HE MATERIALS BELOW provide information about sources cited and other sources with significant information related to topics addressed in this book. Items are listed alphabetically by author or title. Not included in the list of materials are various creeds and statements of faith/belief from different religious groups, even though some of them are mentioned in the book. They are not included because they are easy to find with no more information than the name of the creed or document.

The reader is expected to apply good sense in regard to materials listed below. Even reputable and authoritative sources may have things in them that the reader has reason to think incorrect or out of line with the reader's perspective. Some of the material below and in the notes would not be included in sources and references in most academic books (such items are mainly websites). Such are included here because those items seem to have things that may interest some readers. Links (URLs) are provided for reader convenience as well as for materials only available on-line..

Ante-Nicene Fathers, subtitled *"The Writings of the Fathers Down to A.D. 325,"* ten volume collection (one volume of which is indexes) initially published in 1885. Available on-line from https://en.wiki-source.org/wiki/Ante-Nicene_Fathers. If an early Christian writer cited in the book is not listed individually among these Basic Works, the writing cited can be found in this collection.

Barrett, David B., George T. Kurian, and Todd M. Johnson (eds.), *World Christian Encyclopedia: A Comparative Survey of Churches and Religions in The Modern World*, (2 Volume Set 2nd Edition, 2001).

Barrett, David B. and Todd M. Johnson, *World Christian Trends AD 30-AD2200: Interpreting the annual Christian megacensus—The Demographics of Christian Martyrdom, AD 33-AD 2001*, William

Carey Library, 2001, http://www.gordonconwell.edu/resources/documents/WCT_Martyrs_Extract.pdf accessed November 2017).

Bible Canon (unedited full-text of the 1906 Jewish Encyclopedia) available at http://www.jewishencyclopedia.com/articles/3259-bible-canon (accessed October 2017).

Broadbent, E. H., *The Pilgrim Church: Being Some Account of the Continuance of Churches Practicing the Principles Taught and Exemplified in the New Testament*, Pickering & Inglis, Ltd., 1931. *The Pilgrim Church* is still in print (Gospel Folio Press) and available free on line, from Project Gutenburg and elsewhere.

Brown, Raymond E., *The Sensus Plenior of Sacred Scripture*, Baltimore: St. Mary's University, 1955.

Calvin, John, *Institutes of the Christian Religion* (1536 in Latin; John T. McNeill, editor, translator Ford Lewis Battles, Philadelphia: Westminster Press, 1960).

Chicago Statement on Biblical Application (http://www.alliancenet.org/the-chicago-statement-on-biblical-application) 1986.

Chicago Statement on Biblical Hermeneutics (http://www.bible-researcher.com/chicago2.html) 1982.

Chicago Statement on Biblical Inerrancy with Exposition (http://www.bible-researcher.com/chicago1.html) 1978.

Cole, Simon A., "More than Zero: Accounting for Error in Latent Fingerprint Identification," *Journal of Criminal Law and Criminology*, Vol. 95, Issue 3 (Spring 2005), pp. 985-1078.

Coptic Orthodox Church Network website, "The Allegorical Interpretation of the Scriptures," http://www.copticchurch.net/topics/patrology/schoolofalex/I-Intro/chapter3.html accessed October 2017.

Crisell, W. A., *The Seven Mysteries Revealed to Paul*, https://www.wacriswell.com/sermons/1956/the-seven-mysteries-revealed-to-paul/ accessed November 2017.

Daubert v. Merrell Dow Pharmaceuticals (509 U.S. 579, 593 in 1993), where the United States Supreme Court identified non-definitive criteria for admissible scientific evidence.

Didache, The (also known as *The Teaching of the Twelve Apostles*), http://www.earlychristianwritings.com/didache.html accessed November 2017.

Dimitrov, Tihomir, *50 Nobel Laureates and Other Great Scientists Who Believe in God*, free e-book (developed 1995-2008) http://nobelist.tripod.com/sitebuildercontent/sitebuilderfiles/50-nobelists.pdf accessed October 2017.

Einstein, Albert, *Relativity: The Special and General Theory* (1916), translated by Robert William Lawson (1920), New York: H. Holt and Company.

Filoni, Fernanco, *The Church in Iraq*, The Catholic University of America Press, 2017, translated by Edward Condon.

Gabriel, Vincent, *A Nestorian Canon of Scripture*, December 30, 2013, from https://blogs.ancientfaith.com/onbehalfofall/a-nestorian-canon-of-scripture/ September 2017).

Glotz, Gustave, "The Price of Papyrus in Greek Antiquity," *Annales d'histore* économique *et sociale*, 1929, Vol 1, no. 1 (translated by Mitchell Abidor).

Ioannidis, John P. A., "An Epidemic of False Claims," *Scientific American*, June 1, 2011.

Jenkins, Philip, *The Lost History of Christianity: The Thousand Year Golden Age of the Church in the Middle East, Africa, and Asia – and How It Died*, Harper Collins Publisher, 2008.

Johnson, Ian, *The Souls of China: The Return of Religion After Mao*, Pantheon Books, New York, 2017.

Johnson, Todd M., *Christian Martyrdom: A Global Demographic Assessment*, presented at Notre Dame University, November 2012 (https://icl.nd.edu/assets/84231/the_demographics_of_christian_martyrdom_todd_johnson.pdf).

Josephus, *Antiquities of the Jews* (about 94 A.D.), *Flavius Josephus Against Apion* (about 97 A.D.), and *The Life of Flavius Josephus* (about 99 A.D.). The complete works of Josephus are available from M. A. Hendrickson Publishers (1987).

Koberlein, Brian, "The Dark History of Dark Matter," *Forbes/ Science/#WhoaScience* (https://www.forbes.com/sites/briankober-lein/2016/09/19/the-dark-history-of-dark-matter/#3ee682dc1894 accessed November 2017).

Koukl, Gregory, *The Story of Reality: How the World Began, How It Ends, and Everything Important that Happens in Between*, Zondervan, 2017.

LaSor, William Sanford, "Prophecy, Inspiration, and Sensus Plenior," *Tyndale Bulletin* 29 (1978), pp. 48-60 (http://www.tyn-dalehouse.com/TynBul/Library/TynBull_1978_29_02_Lasor_ ProphecySensusPlenior.pdf accessed September 2017).

Lee, Morgan, "Sorry, Tertullian," *Christianity Today*, December 4, 2014 (http://www.christianitytoday.com/ct/2014/december/sorry-tertul-lian.html).

Lewis, C.S., *The Problem of Pain*, first published in 1940.

Lloyd-Jones, D. Martyn, *Studies in the Sermon on the Mount*, Vol. 1 & 2, Inter-Varsity Fellowship, 1959.

Luther, Martin, *Table Talk*, translated by William Haslitt, 1857.

Maier, Paul L. (ed.), *Eusebius: The Church History; A New Translation with Commentary*, Grand Rapids: Kregel, 1999.

May, Eric, "The Problem of a Biblical Mariology," *Marian Studies*: Vol. 11, Article 6, Pages 21-59 (2016). Available at http://ecommons. udayton.edu/marian_studies/vol11/iss1/6 (accessed October 2017).

Merali, Zeeya, *A Big Bang in a Little Room: The Quest to Create New Universes*, Basic Books, 2017.

Mingana, Alphonse, *The Early Spread of Christianity in Central Asia and the Far East: A New Document*, reprinted from The Bulletin of the John Rylands Library, Vol. 9, No. 2 (1925).

Moo, Douglas J., "The Problem of *Sensus Plenior*" http://patricksch-reiner.com/wp-content/uploads/2012/05/sensusplenior.pdf (accessed September 2017).

Muller, Richard A., *The Physics of Time*, W. W. Norton & Co., 2016.

Nelson, James M., "Estimates of the total number all Christian martyrs in the former Soviet Union are about 12 million", *Psychology, Religion, and Spirituality*, Springer, 2009.

Newman, Andy, "Fingerprinting's Reliability Draws Growing Court Challenges," *The New York Times*, April 7, 2001.

Niebuhr, Reinhold, *The Nature and Destiny of Man*, Vols 1-2, initially published in 1943. Available from various publishers and free on-line.

Origen, *Commentary on the Gospel of Matthew (Book X)*, http://www.newadvent.org/fathers/101610.htm accessed November 2017.

Oss, Douglas A., "Canon as Context: The Function of *Sensus Plenior* in Evangelical Hermeneutics," *Grace Theological Journal* 9.1 (1988), pp. 105-127 (http://www.tyndalehouse.com/TynBul/Library/TynBull_1978_29_02_Lasor_ProphecySensusPlenior.pdf accessed September 2017).

Owen, John, *The Divine Original: Authority, Self-Evidencing Light, and Power of the Scriptures* (17th century).

Popper, Karl, *The Logic of Scientific Discovery* (originally published in 1934, available in an English translation free on line at http://strangebeautiful.com/other-texts/popper-logic-scientific-discovery.pdf (accessed October 2017). Some label the approach of Popper as "empirical falsification."

Raine, Adrian, *The Anatomy of Violence: The Biological Roots of Crime*, Pantheon Books, 2013.

Ryrie, Alec, *Protestants: The Faith That Made the Modern World*, Viking, 2017.

Schaff, Philip, *History of the Christian Church, Volume II: Ante-Nicene Christianity. A.D. 100-325* (first published 1882; http://www.documentacatholicaomnia.eu/03d/1819-1893,_Schaff._Philip,_History_Of_Christian_Church_[02]_Ante-Nicene_ChristianityAD_100-325,_EN.pdf accessed November 2017).

Sherrill, John, Brother Andrew, and Elizabeth Sherrill, *God's Smuggler*, Chosen Books, 2001.

Stark, Rodney. *The Rise of Christianity*. Princeton University Press (1996).

Taylor, David, *21 Signs of His Coming: Major Biblical Prophecies Being Fulfilled In Our Generation*, Taylor Publishing Group, 2009.

Ulery, Bradford T. et al. "Accuracy and Reliability of Forensic Latent Fingerprint Decisions." *Proceedings of the National Academy of Sciences of the United States of America* 108.19 (2011): 7733–7738.

Viviano, Pauline A., "The Senses of Scripture," *National Bible Week 2015* (http://www.usccb.org/bible/national-bible-week/upload/viviano-senses-scripture.pdf accessed September 2017).

Waldron, Samule, *Historical Theology*, Part 2: The Expansion of Christianity, Section 2: Its Preconstantine Expansion, http://www.vor.org/truth/rbst/hist-theology-003.html (accessed November 2017).

Warfield, B. B., *The Inspiration and Authority of the Bible*.

Whitaker, William, *Disputations on Holy Scripture* (16th century).

Young, E. J., *Thy Word Is Truth* (first published 1957).

Notes

1   In the mid-1950s Niebuhr's "Christian Realism" contrasted with liberal theological ideas of the time by contending that such ideas did not deal with the reality of fallen humanity. Niebuhr's ideas drew extensive upon his 1943 publication *The Nature and Destiny of Man*; a work that *Time* and others identify as one of the most significant non-fiction publications of the 20th century.

2   Perspective on reality presented in this book is similar to that of notable believers in God such as Blaise Pascal, Robert Boyle, Isaac Newton, Gregor Mendel, Asa Gray, Lord Kelvin, Max Planck, Arthur Compton, Antoine Suarez, Katharine Hayhoe, and Don Page. This short list from the many that could have been in the list includes those well-known from history (such as Pascal, Newton, and Mendel) and those currently making significant contributions to science (such as Hayhoe's work on climate science, Suarez's work on the foundations of quantum physics, and Page's work on theoretical gravitational physics and cosmology). Similar perspectives on reality were characteristic of those identified in Tihomir Dimitrov's *50 Nobel Laureates and Other Great Scientists Who Believe in God*, free e-book (developed 1995-2008) http://nobelist.tripod.com/sitebuildercontent/sitebuilderfiles/50-nobelists.pdf accessed October 2017.

3   Karl Popper, *The Logic of Scientific Discovery* (originally published in 1934, available in an English translation free on line at http://strangebeautiful.com/other-texts/popper-logic-scientific-discovery.pdf (accessed October 2017). Some label the approach of Popper as "empirical falsification."

4   Richard A. Muller, *The Physics of Time*, W. W. Norton & Co., 2016.

5   Ian Johnson, *The Souls of China: The Return of Religion After Mao* (Pantheon Books, New York, 2017, p. 16). Johnson is an advising

editor for *The Journal of Asian Studies* and teaches a course on religion in Beijing (where he lives).

6   D. Martyn Lloyd-Jones, *Studies in the Sermon on the Mount*, Vol. 1, Inter-Varsity Fellowship, 1959, p.10

7   Brian Koberlein, "The Dark History of Dark Matter," *Forbes/Science/#WhoaScience* (https://www.forbes.com/sites/briankoberlein/2016/09/19/the-dark-history-of-dark-matter/#3ee682dc1894 accessed November 2017).

8   Those unfamiliar with Plato's Cave can read about it in *The Republic* or at web sites such as the Wikipedia article about it (https://en.wikipedia.org/wiki/Allegory_of_the_Cave).

9   If the change of water density with temperature were measured at 10, 15, or even 20 evenly spaced temperatures between the freezing point and boiling point of water, the change in the direction of density change in water with temperature would not be detected.

10   Albert Einstein, *Relativity: The Special and General Theory* (1916), translated by Robert William Lawson (1920), New York: H. Holt and Company.

11   Few people are aware of the many issues related to inflation that modern scientists have been trying to address. Some of the mathematical approaches to inflation suggest it should never stop. Other approaches to it say time does not exist within the universe until it is observed from outside, and some say that the outside observer has to be conscious for time to start working within the universe (implications for an indication of God's role in creation from such are obvious). A delightful discussion of these things along with lots of personal information about scientists involved with these issues can be found in *A Big Bang in a Little Room: The Quest to Create New Universes* (Basic Books, 2017) by Zeeya Merali.

12   Extreme conditions of temperature and pressure seem to exist within the universe and might create exotic states of matter which are non-baryonic. Those extreme conditions might also change some of the processes of chemistry and physics. Such would be similar to what Einstein did with the theory of relativity when he suggested very high speeds impact time and mass. This is an alternative to the

assumption that laws of biology, chemistry, and physics observed currently on earth apply throughout time and space.

13 Dr. Muller received the 2015 Breakthrough prize in fundamental physics for the Supernova Cosmology project.

14 Some of the several thousand members in the International Flat Earth Society are not serious about its purported beliefs but are members for frivolous reasons, such as to agitate others.

15 Although studies of the brain and nervous systems have been done for many centuries, it was only in the 20th century that neuroscience began to be recognized as a distinct academic discipline. The earliest reference for the term "neuroscience" comes from the 1960s when various schools established research programs or departments bringing together biology, chemistry, physics, and mathematics under the label of "neuroscience;" establishment of the Society for Neurosciences occurred about the same time.

16 Challenges to the concept of "free will" exist from cosmology and theology as well as from neuroscience. In theology, the challenge to free will comes from God's predestination of the saved; CCR posits resolution of that as a conundrum of God's infinite nature: both free will and predestination can be true simultaneously because of God's infinite nature. Some perspectives on cosmology have a deterministic concept somewhat similar to predestination, with a similar impact on free will, but quantum theory might provide an opportunity in cosmology for free will. This book makes no attempt to resolve free will issues beyond what is said about that subject theologically. It merely notes that the issue of free will shows up elsewhere as well.

17 The word may have been coined by Adrian Raine, a leading authority on the biology of violence and a professor of Criminology, Psychiatry, and Psychology at the University of Pennsylvania.

18 Details about this case are available in Adrian Raine, *The Anatomy of Violence: The Biological Roots of Crime*, Pantheon Books, 2013.

19 For examples, Andy Newman, "Fingerprinting's Reliability Draws Growing Court Challenges," *The New York Times*, April 7, 2001; Todd Cooper, "Omaha Prosecutors' Memo Delves into Crime Lab Controversies over Suspended Director's Fingerprint Evidence," *Omaha World-Herald*, March 30, 2015.

20 In *Daubert v. Merrell Dow Pharmaceuticals* (509 U.S. 579, 593 in 1993) the United States Supreme Court identified non-definitive criteria for admissible scientific evidence.

21 For example, analysis of the accuracy and reliability of latent print examiners showed 85% of examiners made at least one false negative error (the overall false negative error rate was 7.5%) Ulery, Bradford T. et al. "Accuracy and Reliability of Forensic Latent Fingerprint Decisions." *Proceedings of the National Academy of Sciences of the United States of America* 108.19 (2011): 7733–7738. Similar information had been available in the forensic community for a long time, such as illustrated by Simon A. Cole, "More than Zero: Accounting for Error in Latent Fingerprint Identification," *Journal of Criminal Law and Criminology*, Vol. 95, Issue 3 (Spring 2005), pp. 985-1078.

22 From John Calvin, *Institutes of the Christian* Religion (1.vii.1,2,5), John T. McNeill, editor, translator Ford Lewis Battles, Philadelphia: Westminster Press, 1960.

23 The 1978 *Chicago Statement on Biblical Inerrancy with Exposition* (http://www.bible-researcher.com/chicago1.html) along with the 1982 *Chicago Statement on Biblical Hermeneutics* (http://www.bible-researcher.com/chicago2.html) and the 1986 *Chicago Statement on Biblical Application* (http://www.alliancenet.org/the-chicago-statement-on-biblical-application) provide a full discussion of Biblical inspiration and inerrancy plus related topics endorsed by a large number of evangelical Biblical scholars.

24 There are a variety of opinions about whether the writings mentioned that no longer exist were originally Scripture. Materials appear at times claiming to be one of the mentioned works. For example, several things with Jasper attached to them were mentioned in writings of antiquity (3rd to 6th century), as noted by a Jewish writer in the 13th century; some appeared as books in both the 17th and 18th century. A translation of the 17th century book can be found today; but most Bible scholars do not believe it is the writing referenced in the Old Testament.

25 Josephus, *Against Apion*, Book 1.

26 *Bible Canon* (unedited full-text of the 1906 Jewish Encyclopedia) available at http://www.jewishencyclopedia.com/articles/3259-bible-canon (accessed October 2017).

27 During the era of the Maccabees civil war existed between Jews emphasizing traditional Jewish religion and Hellenized Jews who thought Hellenization would be good for a nation dominated by the Greek Seleucid Empire. During this period, Seleucid Empire policy changed from tolerance of Judaism which had permitted Jews to practice their traditional Jewish religion to efforts to abolish traditional Jewish religion when Antiochus IV Epiphanes began to reign. Most aspects of the Jewish religion were forbidden, the temple was desecrated, and many were killed (including mothers and their young sons because the women had their baby boys circumcised). In addition, there were extensive efforts to destroy copies of the Hebrew Bible. Because of this, it is possible that less than the best copies of the Hebrew Bible survived (and some of what survived may even have been reconstructed from memory). This is why the LXX may represent an older version of the Hebrew Scripture than the Masoretic Text in some passages. Detailed information about such does not exist at this time.

28 Eusebius, *Ecclesiastical History*, Book 3, Chapter 3.

29 There are about a dozen autocephalous churches (each of which is essentially a denomination) in the communions of Eastern, Oriental, and Western Orthodox Churches.

30 Only groups whose canons were established by the time such was done by Christianity in the Roman Empire (4th-5th century) are included. Later additions to Christendom (such as the Mormons or Christian Scientists) are not addressed in discussion of the canon of Scripture; such late-comers often have writings that they consider Scripture, but which the older parts of Christendom do not.

31 Western oriented church histories tend to largely ignore the massive missionary endeavors associated with Nestorian Christianity during the first millennium of the church; they were the ones evangelizing in India and China long before other kinds of Christians reached those peoples. In addition, their attitude toward Scripture may not have been as strict as elsewhere in Christendom. For example, it is claimed that Mar Abd Yeshua (a leader of the Nestorian Church about 1298 A.D.) included in his canon of the Old Testament some things from the LXX and some not in the LXX that are not in the Protestant Old Testament (Vincent Gabriel, *A Nestorian Canon of Scripture*, December 30, 2013, from https://blogs.ancientfaith.

com/onbehalfofall/a-nestorian-canon-of-scripture/ accessed
September 2017).

32 *Codex Sinaiticus* contains the *Epistle of Barnabas* and *The Shepherd
(of Hermas)* as part of its New Testament and the two *Esdras*,
Tobit, Judith, *1ˢᵗ & 4ᵗʰ Maccabees*, *Wisdom*, and *Sirach* from the
Apocrypha. *Codex Vatincanus* contains all of the *Apocrypha* except
1ˢᵗ-4ᵗʰ Maccabees. It is missing *1ˢᵗ & 2ⁿᵈ Timothy*, *Titus*, *Philemon*, and
Revelation; it probably also had contained a few books not included
in our New Testament. *Codex Alexandrinus* contains essentially all
of the *Apocrypha*, *1 Clement* as part of the New Testament, and
various comments on portions of Scripture such as the "Epistle to
Marcellinus" attributed to Saint Athanasius and the Eusebian summary of the Psalms which are inserted before the Book of Psalms.

33 It is difficult to find simple summaries about such things. One has
to examine a number of sources, such as Alphonse Mingana, *The
Early Spread of Christianity in Central Asia and the Far East: A
New Document*, reprinted from The Bulletin of the John Rylands
Library, Vol. 9, No. 2 (1925). Fortunately, there are various summa-
ries of this information, such as in Philip Jenkins, *The Lost History
of Christianity: The Thousand Year Golden Age of the Church in the
Middle East, Africa, and Asia – and How It Died*, Harper Collins
Publisher, 2008.

34 Textual criticism considers such things as date for a manuscript with
the text of a passage, the text of that same passage from manuscripts
in different geographic areas, relation of the text to how that passage
has been translated (with assumptions about the date of the translation), how the style (terminology, grammar, etc.) of a passage fits
with other related material, etc.

35 For example, the Preface for the 2001 English Standard Version
(ESV) states that the ESV Old Testament is based upon the Masoretic
Text of the Hebrew Bible. Consequently its text follows the Masoretic
Text with just a footnote for an alternative reading based upon material in the Dead Sea Scrolls, the LXX, or other early sources. That
approach caused this author to be very disappointed in how the ESV
translated Goliath's height in 1 Samuel 17:4 as "six cubits and a
span;" relegating the superior reading of "four cubits and a span" to
a footnote saying that the Dead Sea Scrolls, the LXX, and Josephus
all say four. To choose the Masoretic Text reading of six over the four

reading from a Hebrew manuscript a thousand years older than the Masoretic text supported by that same reading from the LXX (the Old Testament version quoted by New Testament writers when it differed from the Masoretic Text) and by material from a first century Jewish historian in the Roman Province of Syria reminds one of a famous quote from Ralph Waldo Emerson: "a foolish consistency is the hobgoblin of little minds." Perhaps sometime between the third and ninth century A.D. a Masorete rabbi copying the Hebrew Bible wanted to enhance the image of the ancient Jewish hero and king, David, by making the giant Goliath even more immense (increasing his height from four cubits and a span to six cubits and a span); thus changing the reading of the Hebrew text. In Hebrew both the letter for the number four (Dalet) and the letter for the number six (Vav) are a vertical line with a horizontal part at the top of the line going to the left. They would be easy to confuse (or to change).

36 Martin Luther, *Table Talk* (translated by William Haslitt, 1857).

37 Numerous examples of such can be found for many varieties of Christians in Alec Ryrie's history of Protestants from Luther to the current day: *Protestants: The Faith That Made The Modern World*, Viking 2017.

38 It would be impossible for such numerical agreement to occur (e.g., too few stars are visible to the human eye, a few thousand, and the number of stars currently thought to be in the universe is too large, far more than the total number of people who have ever lived which is a larger number than possible for the people from a single ethnic/racial group). Unfortunately, it is not always easy to determine if a passage should be interpreted literally or figuratively.

39 This is illustrated by studies such as that by Gustave Glotz, "The Price of Papyrus in Greek Antiquity," *Annales d'histore* économique *et sociale*, 1929, Vol 1, no. 1 (translated by Mitchell Abidor).

40 A simple example of such is the following. If a person took a Biblical prophecy from the Old Testament about a specific activity or thing (such as the 70 years of desolation for the land and a return of the people from captivity found in Jeremiah 25:1-11 and 29:1-10) and applied it to a contemporary situation (such as a member of an ethnic group that had been oppressed for a long period might do), then that interpretation certainly would end up violating the meaning of

that prophecy because it had ignored the context of the passage of Scripture.

41 Many trace roots of the allegorical interpretation of the Old Testament by Christians in the early centuries of Christianity to a Hellenistic Jewish philosopher who lived in Alexandria (Egypt) during the time of Christ, Philo of Alexander (~20 B.C. to 50 A.D.).

42 Raymond E. Brown, *The Sensus Plenior of Sacred Scripture* (Baltimore: St. Mary's University, 1955), p. 92.

43 Various people have wrestled with this issue, and some provide helpful guidance, such as found in The 1977 Annual Lecture of the Institute for Biblical Research: William Sanford LaSor, "Prophecy, Inspiration, and Sensus Plenior," *Tyndale Bulletin* 29 (1978), pp. 48-60 (available at http://www.tyndalehouse.com/TynBul/Library/TynBull_1978_29_02_Lasor_ProphecySensusPlenior.pdf accessed September 2017). Similarly helpful is Douglas A. Oss, "Canon as Context: The Function of *Sensus Plenior* in Evangelical Hermeneutics," *Grace Theological Journal* 9.1 (1988), pp. 105-127 (available at http://www.tyndalehouse.com/TynBul/Library/TynBull_1978_29_02_Lasor_ProphecySensusPlenior.pdf accessed September 2017). The article was originally prepared for the doctoral seminar entitled "Hermenutical Foundations," Westminster Theological Seminary, Philadelphia, PA.

44 A fairly full identification of issues involved in "The Problem of *Sensus Plenior*" has been identified by Douglas J. Moo, Assocociate Professor of New Testament at Trinity Evangelical Divinity School (Deerfield, Illinois). It is available at http://patrickschreiner.com/wp-content/uploads/2012/05/sensusplenior.pdf (accessed September 2017).

45 The material was written originally for Catechetical Sunday 2008, copyright held by the United States Conference of Catholic Bishops, Washington, D.C.

46 This is illustrated by "The Allegorical Interpretation of the Scriptures" on the website of the Coptic Orthodox Church Network (http://www.copticchurch.net/topics/patrology/schoolofalex/I-Intro/chapter3.html accessed October 2017).

47 The **Ante-Nicene Fathers**, subtitled *"The Writings of the Fathers Down to A.D. 325"* is a ten volume collection (one volume of which is indexes) containing English translations of the majority of Early Christian writings. The period covers the beginning of Christianity until before the promulgation of the Nicene Creed at the First Council of Nicaea in 325 A.D. The index for Scriptures discussed/commented upon by the different writers during that period (which includes the early church and goes about 80 years beyond it) has no entry for Matthew 2:23. Apparently the only comment in that era related to Matthew 2:23 comes from Book X of Origen's commentary on Matthew. "And Mark says, 'And He came into His own country and His disciples follow Him.' [Mark 6:1] We must therefore inquire whether, by the expression, 'His own country,' is meant Nazareth or Bethlehem—Nazareth, because of the saying, 'He shall be called a Nazarene,' [Matthew 2:23] or Bethlehem, since in it He was born." From Origen's *Commentary on the Gospel of Matthew (Book X)*, http://www.newadvent.org/fathers/101610.htm accessed November 2017.

48 Many assume that only people are made in the image of God. The Scripture clearly states that people are in the image of God, but nowhere does Scripture say ONLY PEOPLE are in the image of God. Assumptions about what God's relationships with other things based upon silence of Scripture may not provide correct perspectives.

49 What is called the Cantor Point Set in this book is called a variety of names, such as the "Cantor Set," "Cantor Ternary Set," or "Cantor Comb." Georg Cantor (1845-1918) is credited with invention of set theory in mathematics. Here is a simple example of the Cantor Point Set that illustrates how it permits a line segment to be thrown away and kept at the same time. Take the line segment between 0 and 1. Throw away its middle third. Then throw away the middle third of each remaining segment, and keep doing that for a very large number of times. If one did this just sixteen times for a finite set of numbers, one would have less than 0.2% of them left (i.e., less than 20 from a thousand!). If one kept throwing away middle thirds of the line segment for many more times, one would essentially throw it all away. But because the line segment between 0 and 1 is infinite instead of finite, the whole thing is still there. A simple explanation of that is if the original line segment were described in a trinary number system, each point on the line segment could be identified by a combination

of 0, 1, & 2. Throwing away middle segments simply removed all points with a 1 in its identification. This left all points which are identified only by combinations of 0 & 2. Since every point in the original line segment could have been described in a binary system by combinations of two items, there is a one-to-one correspondence between what is left and what was there originally before the middle thirds were thrown away. So the line segment that was completely thrown away is still there completely. A conundrum for finite mathematics because of the infinite nature of the line segment.

50 Jonah 3:10 is a classic example of such. God changed His plan and did not destroy the city of Nineveh.

51 Parts of Hebrews in this papyrus manuscript are in the Chester Beatty Biblical Papyri (Dublin, Ireland) and parts are in the University of Michigan Papyrus Collection (Ann Arbor, Michigan).

52 This author's experience as an analyst of national defense issues affects his attitude about comments such as the "great accuracy" one. For example, years ago he was involved in a major study. One of his assignments was to determine what value should be used for a significant parameter of the study and how much confidence could be placed in that value. At first, it looked like an easy thing to determine. A number of government organizations (8-10 different ones) had basically the same value for the parameter. But digging a bit deeper, it became clear that those government organizations drew upon secondary or tertiary sources, not primary sources of information about the parameter. Digging even deeper revealed that everything known about that parameter came from just one test, a test which was poorly documented and may have not been done well. Hence it became clear that what originally appeared to be a significant parameter with a well-established value was actually a significant parameter with a very questionable value. That experience makes one very cautious about statements such as the "great accuracy" one.

53 The first instance of a possible "addition" to God's Word occurred in the Garden of Eden. Before Eve was created, God told Adam, "You may surely eat of every tree of the garden, [17] but of the tree of the knowledge of good and evil you shall not eat, for in the day that you eat of it you shall surely die." (Genesis 2:16-17 ESV) When talking with the serpent later, Eve said, "We may eat of the fruit of the trees in the garden, [3] but God said, 'You shall not eat of the fruit of the tree

that is in the midst of the garden, neither shall you touch it, lest you die.'" (Genesis 3:2-3 ESV) It is unknown whether God had modified the commandment to include no touching of the tree, or it was an addition by Eve or based upon what Adam told her. This author thinks this was the first example of people modifying God's Word by adding to it. If so, it occurred before the disobedience of eating the forbidden fruit.

54 The "Romans Road" is a set of Bible verses from the book of Romans in the New Testament that explains God's plan of salvation: Romans 3:23; 3:10; 5:12; 6:23; 5:8; 10:9-10; and 10:13.

55 For example, this phrase is taken verbatim from *Bible Scripture – God's Instruction Manual for Life*, http://www.faithandhealthconnection.org/bible-scripture/ accessed November 2017.

56 The *Oxford English Dictionary (OED)* gives its initial definition for the word "man" as a noun as "A human being (irrespective of sex or age)" and lists 971 A.D. as date of its first citation with that connotation in English.

57 Usually in such passages, the Hebrew word KANAPH (which basically means "extremity") is the word translated "corner."

58 Contemporary views of science cannot say anything about the majority of the universe (Dark Energy and Dark Matter) beyond that it causes what can be observed not to behave as expected if the unobservable stuff did not exist. Science has nothing but theory to support the idea that any of the processes assumed to be applicable across time and space apply as they are assumed to apply.

59 How many elders attended that meeting is unknown. Likewise unknown is what proportion of congregations in Ephesus they represented, and whether all congregations represented had the same number of elders present. There are no contemporary comments about such (or comments about such from within a generation or two of that meeting).

60 A helpful discussion of this subject is available in a 1956 sermon by Dr. W. A. Criswell, long time pastor of the First Baptist Church in Dallas, Texas. It is *The Seven Mysteries Revealed to Paul*, https://www.wacriswell.com/sermons/1956/the-seven-mysteries-revealed-to-paul/ accessed November 2017.

61 This statement assumes that the Ethiopian eunuch whom Philip baptized (Acts 8:26-40) was Jewish. Otherwise, the Ethiopian eunuch was the first Gentile in the church. The fact that the Ethiopian eunuch was reading from a prophet of the Old Testament (Isaiah) when Philip met him is the primary reason for believing that he was Jewish. That he may have been returning from a visit to Jerusalem for religious reasons is also a possibility if he were Jewish.

62 A noted theologian, Charles Hodge, said this about progressive revelation in Scripture: "The progressive character of divine revelation is recognized in relation to all the great doctrines of the Bible... What at first is only obscurely intimated is gradually unfolded in subsequent parts of the sacred volume, until the truth is revealed in its fulness." *Systematic Theology*, 3 vols., 1872-73. In general, the canon of Christian Scripture was considered closed after the passing of the apostles and their associates. Various groups, such as the Mormons, have materials which they consider Scripture (or other authoritative things such as Sacred Tradition in the Roman Catholic Church that are considered of equal authority to the Scripture). Sometimes the progressive nature of revelation in Scripture is used to justify acceptance of these materials that originated after the passing of the apostles and their associates. Progressive revelation in this book is restricted to material within Christian Scripture. Material outside the canon of the Old and New Testaments is not given Scriptural authority by CCR.

63 Some teach that speaking in tongues is a necessary sign of true conversion because Acts 2:4 says all of the followers of Jesus who were together in one place on the Day of Pentecost were filled with the Holy Spirit and spoke in tongues; however, such speaking in tongues is not said about any of the 3,000 who believed Peter's message that day about Christ and were baptized (Acts 2:41). The description of conversion of Samaritans by the preaching of Philip and their reception of the Holy Spirit through Peter and John has no mention of speaking in tongues (Acts 8:9-25). Nor did the conversion of the Ethiopian eunuch mention speaking in tongues (Acts 8:26-40). Likewise the record of Saul's conversion in Acts 9 mentions him being filled with the Holy Spirit and being baptized; but nothing is said about his speaking in tongues in regard to his conversion. The Philippian jailor was told to believe and be saved. He did and was baptized, but there is no mention in the Acts 16 account of him or

his family speaking in tongues. So the idea that speaking in tongues is a necessary sign of true conversion seems to be at odds with the Scriptural record as well as not being mentioned by Paul in Romans 10:9-10 where he summarizes the salvation process.

64 Details for such may be found in the March 2006 blog of David A. Croteau (http://slaveoftheword.blogspot.com/2006/03/ accessed November 2017). Go to the bottom of the blog and work up from the March 4 blog. Croteau's doctoral dissertation is on this very subject: David A. Croteau, A Biblical and Theological Analysis of Tithing: Toward a Theology of Giving in the New Covenant Era, Ph.D. dissertation December 2005, available at http://digitalcommons.liberty.edu/cgi/viewcontent.cgi?article=1016&context=fac_dis (accessed October 2017).

65 *The Pilgrim Church* is still in print (Gospel Folio Press) and available free on line, from Project Gutenburg and elsewhere.

66 The practices noted concern priests, baptism of infants, and tithing. The vast majority of people in Christendom (well over 80% of them) are in churches or groups which have one or more of those practices. This emphasizes the point that there are few churches or Christian groups whose practices are totally consistent with the New Testament. This book is not advocating particular changes to churches other than to encourage all, especially Christians, to approach reality (including its spiritual aspects) with honesty and candor, encouraging Christians to emulate the spiritual unity of the early church. Suggestions beyond that are outside the scope of this book.

67 In 2005, the author retired from the Principal Professional Staff of The Johns Hopkins University Applied Physics Laboratory, where he had worked for more than three decades as a specialist in operations research.

68 Dr. Muller is a well-known scientist, a professor of physics at the University of California at Berkeley. He received a MacArthur Prize "Genius" fellowship, as well as the National Science Foundation Alan T. Waterman Award "for highly original and innovative research which has led to important discoveries and inventions in diverse areas of physics, including astrophysics, radioisotope dating, and optics." In 2015, he shared in the Breakthough Prize for the Supernova Cosmology project.

69 Ryrie's 500 years of Protestant history (*Protestants*, Viking 2017) show repeated emphasis on church self-interest and privileges when dealing with adverse political environments such as European religious wars, Hitler's Germany, slavery era America, apartheid in South Africa, etc.; that focus often allowed other issues to be largely ignored, even very significant ones.

70 "Blue laws" are laws prohibiting (or requiring) various behaviors (such as church attendance or avoiding commerce on Sunday). They predate our becoming a nation; they began in the colonial period. Many blue laws were removed from the books in the U.S. by mid-20th century. Canada inherited Sunday prohibition of work and entertainment in 1763 when it became an English colony and then in the 19th century passed its own laws about such. Contrary to popular tradition, the name "blue laws" probably does not come from the laws being written on blue paper but from the connotation of "rigid moral standard" for the word "blue" in colonial days and the 18th century.

71 The Christians in Hitler's Germany struggled with this in the 1930s and 1940s. The complex history of the decade-plus from Hitler's rise to leadership of Germany to the end of World War II illustrates the different ways that Christians wrestled with the situation and consequences for many of them.

72 A major consequence of this behavior of the 431 A.D. Council of Ephesus was the split of the collection of Orthodox churches from Western Christendom of the Roman Catholic Church.

73 The competing religions included elements of Judaism rejecting the Messiah (Christ) Jesus ; the various gods worshipped by the Egyptians, Greeks, and Romans; and other local religions.

74 Heresies faced by the early church included Legalism (the idea that something people do is required to merit salvation from God, such as circumcision which Judaizers stressed), Docetism (the idea that Jesus Christ did not have a real body), Marcionism (the idea that the God of the Old Testament was not the same as the God of Jesus), Montanism (a movement that gave ecstatic utterances by the followers of Montanus, especially by women, the same authority as given to the Gospels), and Gnosticism (it promoted an extreme dualism, drawing a distinction between the body and the spirit realm with progress through various levels of the spirit realm requiring

special knowledge not possessed by most people. The heresies just mentioned had substantial followings in the early church, but they were not the only ones distorting God's truth in that era. For example, in Jesus' letter to the church at Pergamum (Revelation 2:12-17) He says they have among them some holding to the teaching of Balaam (i.e., eating food sacrificed to idols and practicing sexual immorality) and some following the teachings of the Nicolaitans (which are not precisely revealed by extant materials, the earliest post-Biblical references to the Nicolaitans come from Irenaeus, Clement of Alexandria, and Tertullian nearly a century later). Such distortions as these of God's truth did not have as widespread acceptance as the heresies previously mentioned, although Revelation 2 indicates the Nicolaitans were also around Ephesus.

75 God also redeemed people before that Day of Pentecost. The focus of this discussion is on God's work through the church; so it focuses only on the era in which the church is present.

76 The Moravian missionaries were the first large-scale Protestant missionary movement. They sent out the first missionaries when there were only 300 inhabitants in Herrnhut (on land of Count Zinzendorf, where basically the movement previous based upon the Unitas Fratrum followers of John Hus was transformed in 1727 into the Moravian Brethren). Within 30 years, the Moravian Brethren had sent hundreds of Christian missionaries to many parts of the world, including the Caribbean, North America (including missions to Native Americans, such as the Mohawks), South America, the Arctic (Greenland), Africa, and the Far East (India and China). Some have estimated that perhaps a missionary went abroad from every 25-30 members of the Moravian Brethren during the 18th century. They were the first in the second millennium of church history to send lay people (rather than only clergy) as missionaries, the first Protestant denomination to minister to slaves, and the first Protestant presence in many countries. They also established a prayer watch of continuous prayer which ran uninterrupted, 24 hours a day, for 100 years.

77 There are no reliable statistics about the number of martyrs in the early church. Most persecution of Christians during the Early Church was at the hands of local authorities and mobs. In addition, no statistics were preserved about the number of Christians slain by persecution instigated by Roman leadership (as by the Emperor Nero in the 60s A.D.). Eusebius is called the father of church history. The

introduction to his church history says Eusebius had found no previous histories, only writings of some about events of their time. He
wrote as leader of the church in Caesarea, location of the most extensive collection of Christian materials at that time (materials which
had been amassed by Origin, a prominent Christian theologian of the
third century, roughly at the end of the Early Church). Eusebius said
"great multitudes" of Christians had been martyred. He knew the hor-
rors of that himself. During the empire-wide persecution by Emperor
Diocletian, both Eusebius and his teacher/mentor Pamphilus were
imprisoned; Eusebius managed to avoid execution but Pamphilus
was martyred.

78 Morgan Lee, "Sorry, Tertullian," *Christianity Today*, December 4,
    2014 (http://www.christianitytoday.com/ct/2014/december/sorry-ter-
    tullian.html).

79 *Christian Martyrdom: A Global Demographic Assessment*, presented
    at Notre Dame University, November 2012 by Todd M. Johnson,
    Director of the Center for the Study of Global Christianity at Gordon-
    Conwell Theological Seminary (https://icl.nd.edu/assets/84231/the_
    demographics_of_christian_martyrdom_todd_johnson.pdf).

80 This portion of the world's population in Christendom comes from
    multiple sources, all of which put it at about a third. Sources include
    the PEW-Templeton Global Religious Futures Project and the *Annual
    Table of World Religions 1900-2025* from the World Network of
    Religious Futurists (http://www.wnrf.org/cms/statuswr.shtml
    accessed November 2017).

81 The numbers themselves are helpful. It is estimated that 35 million or
    so Christian martyrs died in the 20th century; that number is far larger
    than the 6 million Jews killed in the Holocaust or the million killed
    in the Rwandan genocide. It has been estimated that the number
    of Christian victims under the Soviet regime was 12-20 million
    ("*Estimates of the total number all Christian martyrs in the former
    Soviet Union are about 12 million.*", James M. Nelson, *Psychology,
    Religion, and Spirituality*, Springer, 2009, ISBN 0387875727, p. 427;
    "*In all, it is estimated that some 15 to 20 million Christians were
    martyred under the Soviet regime*", David Barrett; *World Christian
    Trends*, Pasadena: William Carey Library, 2001, cited by David
    Taylor, *21 Signs of His Coming: Major Biblical Prophecies Being
    Fulfilled In Our Generation*, Taylor Publishing Group, 2009, ISBN

097629334X, p. 220; and *"over 20 million were martyred in Soviet prison camps"*, Todd M. Johnson, *Christian Martyrdom: A global demographic assessment*, p. 4). It is not possible to estimate reliably the number martyred in Red China during Chairman Mao's time, but it was a very large number.

82 If one adds all the numbers for followers of Jesus in the Gospels and the early chapters of Acts, perhaps the followers of Jesus in the church initially might represent about 1% of the Jews in the Roman Province of Syria.

83 Samuel Waldron, *Historical Theology*, Part 2: The Expansion of Christianity, Section 2: Its Pre-Constantine Expansion, http://www.vor.org/truth/rbst/hist-theology-003.html (accessed November 2017). Philip Schaff in his monumental *History of the Christian Church, Volume II: Ante-Nicene Christianity. A.D. 100-325* (first published 1882: http://www.documentacatholicaomnia.eu/03d/18191893,_Schaff._Philip,_History_Of_Christian_Church_[02]_Ante-Nicene_ChristianityAD_100-325,_EN.pdf accessed November 2017) notes that in the absence of statistics the number of Christians at the time is a matter of conjecture, and then states that by 300 A.D. it was likely 10-12% (or more) of the Roman Empire were Christians (p.19). Such an estimate is compatible with the assessment by sociologist Rodney Stark that Christianity grew by about 40% per decade for its first 2-3 centuries, *The Rise of Christianity*, Princeton University Press, 1996.

84 Armenia was the first country to adopt Christianity as its official religion, in the early 4th century. Adoption of Christianity as the official religion of the Roman Empire occurred more than half a century later. The Armenian church claims to have originated in the missions of Apostles Bartholomew and Thaddeus in the 1st century.

85 In antiquity it took a long time for people and messages to go from one place to another (by foot, caravan, sail boat, etc.). Writing materials were expensive (according to a 1929 article by Gustave Glotz, "The Price of Papyrus in Greek Antiquity," it probably took much of a day's wage for a common person to purchase a page or two of papyrus outside Egypt during the early church) and literacy was low (10-20% by most estimates) so most people only got exposed to Scripture and writings from Christian leaders by such being read aloud in religious services or at other group meetings.

86 All deities in the Roman, Greek, Egyptian, and Indian pantheons as well as others worshipped in a locality (and elements of Judaism that rejected the Messiah Jesus) competed with Christianity for attention and allegiance of people in a locality.

87 Heresies faced by the early church with the largest following were Legalism, Docetism, Marcionism, Montanism, and Gnosticism. Other distortions of God's truth also existed (such as the Nicolaitans) but are not thought to have had the widespread acceptance possessed by the heresies named here.

88 It is estimated that more than 30,000 Christian denominations now exist. *World Christian Encyclopedia: A Comparative Survey of Churches and Religions in The Modern World*, (2 Volume Set 2nd Edition, 2001), editors: David B. Barrett, George T. Kurian, and Todd M. Johnson.

89 Such becomes a major problem later (a century or so after the early church as defined herein) when Christianity became acceptable as a religion within the Roman Empire (early 4th century) and then as the only acceptable religion within the Roman Empire (late 4th century). It continues to be a problem when Christianity is associated with a nation as its religion; and it also is a problem at a far lesser scale in squabbles over religious property or assets by a congregation or denomination.

90 Information from the Early Church is inadequate for estimation of the number martyred to be more than a guess, but 10% seems compatible with ancient comments (such as "great multitudes" by Eusebius in his church history) and the massive collection of information in Barrett and Johnson's *Demographics of Christian Martyrdom, AD 33-AD 2001* at http://www.gordonconwell.edu/resources/documents/WCT_Martyrs_Extract.pdf.

91 A good approach to identifying the Elect assumes: 1) the Elect profess faith in the God of the Christian Scripture and trust what Jesus has done on the cross and in His resurrection as the only reason God will forgive their sins and give them eternal life, and 2) their lives consistently manifest the fruit of the Spirit (Galatians 5:22-23: love, joy, peace, patience, kindness, goodness, faithfulness, gentleness, self-control). Without consistent manifestation of the fruit of

the Spirit in a person's life, words about the person's beliefs do not carry much weight.

92 Fernando Filoni is a Cardinal of the Roman Catholic Church and has been Prefect of the Congregation for the Evangelization of Peoples in the Roman Curia since his appointment by Pope Benedict XVI on 10 May 2011. Cardinal Filoni is an expert in Chinese affairs and on the Middle East, having been the formal diplomatic representative from the Vatican to several places, including Iraq and Jordan 2001-2006.

93 It is (or was) located in Dura-Europos in Syria. It was apparently a normal domestic house converted for worship sometime between 233 and 256 A.D. Status of the church structure is unknown after occupation by ISIS; fortunately its famous frescos were removed after discovery of the building in the 1930s and are now preserved at Yale University Art Gallery.

94 The traditional view is that only Jesus and the Twelve were present at the Last Supper, but Acts 1:21-26 suggests that others may have been there too since the candidates for replacement of Judas were said to have been with them "all the time" from the beginning of Christ's public ministry to qualify as "a witness to His resurrection." Perhaps Jesus and the Twelve were at the head table and others were at other places in the room. Some think the "upper room" mentioned in Acts 1 where the followers of Jesus came after His ascension was the location for both the Last Supper and where the followers of Jesus were when they appointed Matthias to be the replacement for Jesus; that location (if all of Acts 1:12-26 occurred in the same location) apparently was large enough to hold 120. It is possible that Jesus meant more by His reference to "them" than the Twelve minus Judas in John 17:20-21; however, since the others would be covered by the ones believing from their words, it is an issue of no significance.

95 Catholic churches have the same kind of splintering as Protestant churches. There are more than fifty religious groups identifying themselves as "Catholic Churches" that are not affiliated with or recognized by the Catholic Church led by the pope in Rome. These groups include the American Catholic Church in the United States, the Old Catholic Church in Europe and of America, the Celtic Catholic Church, the Brazilian Catholic Apostolic Church, the Ukrainian Orthodox Greek Catholic Church, etc.

96 Perhaps for some being "Christian" as a Catholic is more a form of social/cultural identity rather than a spiritual reality based upon a faith commitment by the person to the Lord Jesus Christ. The reader can decided whether to call a person a "Christian" who was baptized as an infant in a Christian church but never makes a profession of faith in Christ, does not attend church services, and lives in disregard of Scriptural guidance.

97 There is a specific reason the examples come only from ministries led by non-government organizations. That reason is the following. Government-employed chaplains are under legal obligation to facilitate service opportunities for all religions claimed by inmates and/or represented in the community about the institution and approved by the governmental authority. Putting aside whatever might be done with non-Christian religions and only addressing Christian activities under the chaplain's leadership, the chaplain has a legal obligation to accept ministry from every variety of Christianity (only restricting such on the basis of security concerns or logistic considerations such as allocating space and scheduling relative to the level of inmate affiliation with such a religion). Some institutions require Christian services to be broad and non-denominational, prohibiting particular denominational or doctrinal emphasis. In dealing with the plethora of Christian groups, a chaplain's program may involve many of them, but typically each group will be doing its own thing without involvement of other groups. Such in itself gives no indication of spiritual unity or its lack. Hence such situations are not addressed in this appendix.

98 Raymond E. Brown, *The Sensus Plenior of Sacred Scripture* (Baltimore: St. Mary's University, 1955), p. 92.

99 Various people have wrestled with this issue, and some provide helpful guidance, such as found in The 1977 Annual Lecture of the Institute for Biblical Research: William Sanford LaSor, "Prophecy, Inspiration, and <u>Sensus Plenior</u>," *Tyndale Bulletin* 29 (1978), pp. 48-60 (available at <u>http://www.tyndalehouse.com/TynBul/ Library/TynBull_1978_29_02_Lasor_ProphecySensusPlenior.pdf</u> accessed September 2017). Similarly helpful is Douglas A. Oss, "Canon as Context: The Function of *Sensus Plenior* in Evangelical Hermeneutics," *Grace Theological Journal* 9.1 (1988), pp. 105-127 (available at <u>http://www.tyndalehouse.com/TynBul/Library/ TynBull_1978_29_02_Lasor_ProphecySensusPlenior.pdf</u> accessed

September 2017). The article was originally prepared for the doctoral seminar entitled "Hermenutical Foundations," Westminster
Theological Seminary, Philadelphia, PA.

100 How Orthodox Christians and others outside of Protestant and
Catholic circles approach *sensus plenior* is not addressed in this book.

101 This point is clear from Eric May (2016), "The Problem of a
Biblical Mariology," *Marian Studies*: Vol. 11, Article 6, Pages 21-59.
Available at http://ecommons.udayton.edu/marian_studies/vol11/
iss1/6 (accessed October 2017). It is part of the *Catholic Studies
Commons, Christianity Commons,* and the *Religious Thought,
Theology and Philosophy of Religious Commons* maintained by the
University of Dayton.

102 A fairly full identification of issues involved in "The Problem of
Sensus Plenior" has been presented by Douglas J. Moo, Assocociate
Professor of New Testament at Trinity Evangelical Divinity School
(Deerfield, Illinois). It is available at http://patrickschreiner.
com/wp-content/uploads/2012/05/sensusplenior.pdf (accessed
September 2017).

103 The material was written originally for Catechetical Sunday 2008,
copyright held by the United States Conference of Catholic Bishops,
Washington, D.C.

104 "Blue laws" are laws prohibiting (or requiring) various behaviors
(such as church attendance or avoiding commerce on Sunday). They
predate the U.S. becoming a nation; they began in the colonial period.
Many blue laws were removed from the books in the U.S. by mid-20th
century. Canada inherited Sunday prohibition of work and entertainment in 1763 when it became an English colony and then in the 19th
century passed its own laws about such. Contrary to popular tradition,
the name "blue laws" probably does not come from the laws being
written on blue paper but from the connotation of "rigid moral standard" for the word "blue" in colonial days and the 18th century.

CPSIA information can be obtained
at www.ICGtesting.com
Printed in the USA
FFOW02n0601100318
45627310-46459FF

9 781545 624272